Modeling and Measuring the Effects of Economic Shocks on a Defense Industrial Base

ELIZABETH HASTINGS ROER, BRENT THOMAS, GRANT JOHNSON, SEAN MCKENNA, NATHANIEL EDENFIELD, CHAD J. R. OHLANDT

Prepared for the Defense Advanced Research Projects Agency
Approved for public release; distribution unlimited

NATIONAL DEFENSE RESEARCH INSTITUTE

For more information on this publication, visit **www.rand.org/t/RRA475-1**.

Published by the RAND Corporation, Santa Monica, Calif.
© 2022 RAND Corporation
RAND® is a registered trademark.

Library of Congress Cataloging-in-Publication Data is available for this publication.

ISBN:978-1-9774-0779-5

Cover: Devrimb/gettyimages.

About This Report

Economic shocks are unanticipated changes in the conditions upon which resource allocation decisions are based. The concern underlying this report is the possibility that economic shocks could induce the same effects as classic kinetic supply interdiction efforts: the degradation of reliable military capability, the diversion of resources from high-priority military initiatives, and the imposition of costs. The purpose of this report is to identify opportunities for improving analytic support to decisionmakers responsible for managing the effects of economic shocks on defense postures. Based on our research findings, we recommend that the Defense Advanced Research Projects Agency (DARPA) or another defense entity invest in a program for advancing data-informed management of economic shocks.[1]

The research reported here was completed in August 2021 and underwent security review with the sponsor and the Defense Office of Prepublication and Security Review before public release.

RAND National Security Research Division

This research was sponsored by DARPA and conducted within the Acquisition and Technology Policy (ATP) Center of the RAND National Security Research Division (NSRD), which operates the National Defense Research Institute (NDRI), a federally funded research and development center sponsored by the Office of the Secretary of Defense, the Joint Staff, the Unified Combatant Commands, the Navy, the Marine Corps, the defense agencies, and the defense intelligence enterprise.

For more information on the RAND ATP Center, see www.rand.org/nsrd/atp.html or contact the director or contact the director (contact information is provided on the webpage).

---

[1] As a federally funded research and development center, RAND NDRI is not eligible to serve as a performer on contracts conducting research for such a program.

Abstract

Economic shocks are unanticipated changes in the conditions upon which resource allocation decisions are based. Economic shocks can include a wide range of events, from typhoons to trade policy changes to mergers and acquisitions—any event that causes a decisionmaker to reconsider such choices as what to buy or sell, how much work to do, what production technology to use, or what price to pay or charge. The concern underlying this report is the possibility that economic shocks could induce the same effects as classic kinetic supply interdiction efforts: the degradation of reliable military capability, the diversion of resources from high-priority military initiatives, and the imposition of costs. The purpose of this report is to assist U.S. Department of Defense (DoD) decisionmakers called upon to respond to those adverse economic shocks by identifying opportunities for improving analysis of shocks and their effects on U.S. defense postures. The authors examined several historical and hypothetical instances in which shocks threatened or would threaten defense postures to identify the types of questions that an analytic capability would ideally be able to answer. They also reviewed data analysis methods used in the economics literature on shocks and evaluated the extent to which these methods provide the desired analytic capability. Research findings suggest that DoD might benefit from improving its capability to analyze shocks. Moreover, although existing methods from economics provide insights necessary for achieving the desired analytic capability, they are not sufficient for fully providing that capability. Novel techniques employing multidisciplinary approaches appear best suited to help close gaps between existing and desired analytic capability, but additional research is needed to develop and refine such techniques.

Summary

Issue

Economic shocks are unanticipated changes in the conditions upon which resource allocation decisions are based. Economic shocks can include a wide range of events, from typhoons to changes in trade policy to mergers and acquisitions—any event that causes a decisionmaker to reevaluate choices such as what to buy or sell, how much work to do, what production technology to use, or what price to pay or charge. The effects of shocks can cascade through economies, markets, and supply chains. Economic shocks can potentially degrade military capability by restricting supply, forcing the diversion of resources from high-priority military objectives to manage the shock, or otherwise imposing costs.

A key assertion underlying this report is that although globalized markets for goods, services, and financial capital can expose countries throughout the world to a similar set of shocks, the United States, its allies, and its adversaries might be differentially exposed to damaging consequences because each country has a distinct economic structure. Consequently, under certain conditions, an economic shock might impart an asymmetric military advantage by more severely affecting some countries' defense industrial bases (DIBs) and economies.

We propose that three sets of features drive the effects of economic shocks on military capability: features of the shock event itself, features of the DIB under consideration, and features related to the response and adaptation of affected entities. From this perspective, managing the effects of economic shocks on the generation of DIB capability is facilitated by an understanding of the sensitivity of outcomes to these features and by subsequently developing interventions for influencing key malleable features.

Yet several technical challenges pose obstacles to leveraging available data to measure system sensitivity. We identified four such challenges.

1. It can be difficult to identify the mathematical structure of the relationship between shock outcomes and features.

2. It can be difficult to distinguish between meaningful measurements and statistical noise, or random variation.
3. The relationships between shock outcomes and features can change over time, especially as decisionmakers in economies, markets, and supply chains adapt over time to earlier shocks.
4. It can be difficult to assess whether relationships are measured with sufficient accuracy to support decisionmaking.

The purpose of this study is to assist U.S. Department of Defense (DoD) decisionmakers who have been called upon to manage the consequences of economic shocks by identifying opportunities for improving analysis of shocks and their effects on U.S. defense postures.

Approach

We framed our research by focusing on several core questions:

- What are the questions of interest that defense decisionmakers need to have addressed to manage the effects of economic shocks on defense postures?
- What are today's methods for modeling these shocks and their effects?
- What are the benefits, challenges, and limits of addressing the questions of interest with today's methods?
- What would a new approach look like, and what types of efforts are needed to achieve a new approach?

To approach these interrelated questions, the research employed several lines of effort.

- We analyzed several *vignettes*—historical and hypothetical instances in which shocks threatened defense postures—to develop a preliminary list of *analytic capability requirements* for supporting DoD decisionmakers.
- We conducted an in-depth review of the economics literature on shocks to assess the extent to which existing methodologies might satisfy DoD analytic capability requirements.

- We conducted an analysis of the gaps between the capabilities requirements and capabilities provided by existing methodologies to better understand what additional development is needed to enhance analytic support to DoD decisionmakers.
- We developed a *construct*—a modular framework that can be tailored to each applied environment—that we propose can help close the identified gaps. We focused our development efforts on the analytic challenges associated with supply restriction—an especially relevant potential consequence of economic shocks.
- Throughout the course of this research, we leveraged a fourth line of effort—a case study—to ensure that our findings were grounded in an understanding of real-world application. The case study illustrates in a recent historical setting how existing empirical methods might provide valuable insights to U.S. policymakers. The case study also elucidates how a framework would help overcome the challenges and limits of existing empirical methods.

Findings

Our exploratory research yielded five key findings:

1. Our analysis of the vignettes suggests that economic shocks have the potential to cause meaningful damage to defense postures, including the degradation of defense capability generation by the DIB.
2. A modest portfolio of analytic capability requirements would support data-informed management of a wide range of concerns created by economic shocks. We identified three distinct sets of issues that characterize the challenges of each of the vignettes: supply restriction, the potential to infer otherwise hidden government priorities, and the potential for extreme responses to economic shocks. We developed a preliminary list of *analytic capability requirements* to support management of each of these challenges and found striking similarity across the vignettes in capabilities that decisionmakers might value.

3. The economics literature on shocks predominantly employs four empirical methods (*workhorse methods*) useful for informing many central questions underlying the analytic capability requirements: vector autoregression, input-output, computable general equilibrium, and panel regression models. These four methods provide many—but not all—of the analytic capabilities that defense decisionmakers might find helpful for data-informed shock management. These four methods analyze shocks from different perspectives and combine to "paint a picture" of possible shock outcomes.

4. We identified an important gap: Existing empirical methods cannot always overcome the technical challenges of achieving the analytic capability requirements. Reliable outputs from any empirical method require data that might not always be available, and assumptions might not always be realistic. Moreover, we found that the selection, construction, and calibration of empirical analysis depend on details of the applied environment, precluding "plug-and-play" analysis; analyses must be tailored to each application.

5. We identified a second important gap: Additional analysis beyond the type of system parameter estimation provided by the workhorse empirical methods is needed to fully exploit the potential of data analysis to support defense decisionmakers. Aside from the question of how to best conduct empirical analyses, the vignettes prompted two additional questions: What empirical analyses should be conducted, and what do the outputs of empirical analyses suggest about the courses of action under consideration?

Preliminary Decision Support Tool

We developed a preliminary tool for closing the identified gaps and improving analytic support to decisionmakers: a framework that can be tailored to a given shock instance and that connects analytic outputs to the options under consideration for managing shock consequences. The frameworks we propose are modular constructs that capture the decision-relevant mechanisms affecting shock instigation, propagation, and effects.

We developed a preliminary and partial framework for shock-induced supply restriction, depicted in Figure S.1. Entities that might be affected by an economic shock can take actions to avoid it or to mitigate and recover from its disruptive effects. But such response and adaptation entails several substeps, which we represent by drawing upon the construct of the observe, orient, decide, act (OODA) loop used in a variety of applications, such as military command and control. Completing each step of the OODA loop takes resources and time. Consequently, the effects of an economic shock depend critically on the outcome of a race between the shock's propagation and the response and adaptation processes of affected entities: The faster potentially affected entities can detect and appropriately respond to the shock, the less damage will be suffered. DIB production process characteristics, such as production time and supply chain structure, mediate the speed of both shock propagation and entity response and adaptation.

The model partitions shock events into three categories for subsequent analysis: Short-latency shocks can potentially affect ongoing combat operations; long-latency shocks are most relevant in long-term competition, affecting production capabilities and technology; and, finally, intermediate-latency shocks sit between these two extremes. We suspect that the outcome of the race between shock propagation and response and adaptation is most "competitive" for intermediate-latency shocks in the sense that the extent to which shock effects outpace response outcomes is most sensitive to variation in the production process characteristics, such as those identified in Figure S.1. For instance, if geopolitical events lead to military buildup or mobilization, a concurrent economic shock might influence, or even decide, outcomes of the subsequent conflict. This might be especially true if some combatant nations are less exposed to the shock, are more resilient to the shock, or are able to more quickly respond due to shorter OODA loops.

Recommendations

Our synthesis of the above research findings leads us to offer two recommendations. First, we recommend that the Defense Advanced Research Projects Agency (DARPA) or another defense entity invest in a program

FIGURE S.1

A Preliminary Time-Based Framework for Shock-Induced Supply Restrictions

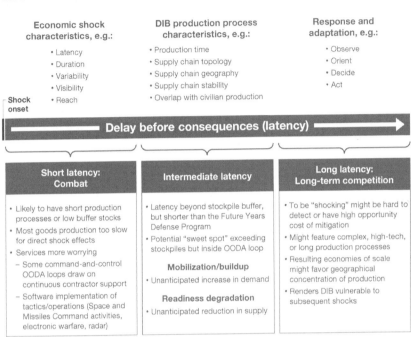

for advancing data-informed management of economic shocks.[2] Economic shocks pose substantial risks to defense postures, and our findings suggest that there might be cost-effective ways to leverage existing empirical methods to improve analytic support to decisionmakers charged with managing these risks. Evidence suggests that some capability requirements could be met through straightforward application of existing empirical methods. On the other hand, achieving other analytic capability requirements will require substantially more investment. The recommended research program should include experts from academia, industry, and the defense establishment across an array of disciplines, potentially including econom-

---

[2]   As a federally funded research and development center, the RAND National Defense Research Institute is not eligible to serve as a performer on contracts conducting research for such a program.

ics, political science, organizational behavior, sociology, military studies (strategy and planning), and defense operations and command. DARPA's program performers could start by developing capabilities with the broadest applicability or lowest investment cost—the "low-hanging fruit"—to both achieve early operational gains and build a base of knowledge that will be helpful for addressing more-challenging capability requirements. We hope that this report provides a helpful starting point in such an effort by making progress on an important first step: defining and structuring the problem.

Second, we recommend that the design and execution of such a program be grounded in specific policy questions or management decisions. Starting with the end in sight can lower performance requirements for empirical analysis by focusing analysis on the boundaries between decision alternatives. Grounding program execution in specific analytic decisions can support successful program outcomes by focusing on central modeling features, such as the data environment, the time horizon over which analytic insights are needed, and relevant shock mechanisms. A way to implement this recommendation is to focus each program increment on a set of historical and hypothetical scenarios carefully selected to approach a specific technical challenge from different relevant angles, such as different data environments, defense capabilities, and industrial structures.

Contents

Figures and Tables

Figures

Tables

Acknowledgments

The research question addressed in this report was conceived by John Paschkewitz, who was a Defense Advanced Research Projects Agency program manager at the time this research was initiated. We are grateful for his foresight in sponsoring this project and for his thoughtful support throughout its duration. We are also grateful to Schuyler Porche and Kristina Sembower of U.S. Strategic Command's Joint Warfare Analysis Center and to Sam Stein, Braden Harker, and Michael Morgan of the Defense Logistics Agency's Office of Strategic Materials for their support, insightful conversation, and productive engagement at various stages of this project.

We are also grateful to our colleagues at RAND. We thank John Birkler, Peter Dortmans, Roger Lough, Richard Silberglitt, and Jonathan Wong, who spent significant time considering and discussing potential vignettes with us, and Varun Chandorkar for assistance translating Iranian input-output tables to English. We thank Steven Popper, Michael Kennedy, Marjory Blumenthal, Caolionn O'Connell, and Christopher Mouton, as well as Ed Keating at the Congressional Budget Office, for their valuable insight, guidance, and feedback. We are thankful to Sydne Newberry for her help improving the clarity of our presentation of this research and its findings.

This project was completed in the Acquisition and Technology Policy Center within the RAND National Security Research Division. We are grateful to Joel Predd, center director, and Yun Kang, associate program director, for their constructive feedback and advice.

CHAPTER ONE

Introduction

In mid-August 1914, the German East Asiatic Squadron deployed the light cruiser *SMS Emden* under the command of Captain Karl von Müller to the Western Pacific and Indian oceans to disrupt the trade routes of its World War I (WWI) adversaries, particularly between England and its colonies.[1] The target was not just Allied war supplies, but also general commerce. Over three months from the start of the war until it was defeated in battle, the *Emden* captured 23 vessels, costing the British an estimated £5,000,000 in damages—over $800 million in 2020 U.S. dollars—a figure 15 times more than the cost to build the *Emden*.[2] The *Emden*'s exploits are credited with inducing panic in the region, halting British shipping from Indian ports, and rapidly increasing insurance costs for ships.[3] Aside from the direct costs of its interdiction activity, the *Emden*'s activities also diverted Allied efforts from elsewhere to secure supply and trade routes in the region: At one point, 78 warships were searching for it. Meanwhile, at least four of the captured ships were converted to support the German war efforts. The *Emden*'s measurable adverse effects on Allied war efforts emboldened similar cost-imposing efforts by Germany across the world.

---

[1] Unless otherwise noted, information in this paragraph is from Christopher Miskimon, "How the German Cruiser *Emden* Terrorized Allied Shipping in World War I," *The National Interest*, March 5, 2020.

[2] Dan Van der Vat, *Gentlemen of War: The Amazing Story of Captain Karl von Müller and the SMS Emden*, New York: Morrow, 1984, p. 119.

[3] Desmond Woods, "Occasional Paper 91: Invidious Choices—The German East Asia Squadron and the RAN in the Pacific, August to December 1914," Naval Historical Society of Australia, October 6, 2020.

Supply interdiction is a tool of warfare that is so long-standing and widespread that specific instances are described among the earliest historical records of wars across several civilizations.[4] Closer to the present, the *Emden* was but one particularly effective commerce raider in a broad portfolio of German efforts to disrupt its adversaries' trade routes, an even more well-known example being Germany's U-boats.[5] World War II (WWII) offers its own examples, such as large-scale efforts by combatants on both sides to disrupt their enemies' oil and rubber supplies, with profound consequences for the course of the war.[6]

Historically, supply interdiction has typically been achieved through kinetic means—through the application of military force. Often, the targets of supply interdiction efforts have been military logistical assets, such as convoys and transportation routes. But other times, efforts have focused on the potentially "softer" target of civilian commerce. As illustrated by the example of the *Emden,* the goal of targeting civilian commerce is not just

---

[4]   In the 8th century BCE, the Assyrian Empire, with the world's first known standing armies, cut off cities' supply lines as it laid siege to it adversaries across Mesopotamia (Davide Nadali, "Sieges and Similes of Sieges in the Royal Annals: The Conquest of Damascus by Tiglath-Pileser III," *Kaskal*, Vol. 6, No. 13, 2009). Centuries later, Rome and Carthage returned blows against overland supply routes, ports, and operational bases loaded with supplies during the Punic Wars (Jonathan P. Roth, *The Logistics of the Roman Army at War*, Leiden, Netherlands: Brill, 1998). Half a world over, in the 17th century, the early Qing Dynasty imposed a maritime trade ban to stop the flow of supplies to resistance elements on Taiwan seeking to reclaim mainland China (Yew Seng Tai, Patrick Daly, E. Edwards Mckinnon, Andrew Parnell, R. Michael Feener, Jedrzej Majewski, Nazli Ismail, and Kerry Sieh, "The Impact of Ming and Qing Dynasty Maritime Bans on Trade Ceramics Recovered from Coastal Settlements in Northern Sumatra, Indonesia," *Archaeological Research in Asia*, Vol. 21, March 2020).

[5]   For more information regarding the role of U-boats in WWI, including their role as commerce raiders, see, for example, Uboat.net, "U-Boat War in World War One," webpage, undated; Esri and Li Zhou, "This Map Shows the Full Extent of the Devastation Wrought by U-Boats in World War I," *Smithsonian Magazine*, May 7, 2015; Javier Ponce, "Commerce Warfare in the East Central Atlantic During the First World War: German Submarines Around the Canary Islands, 1916–1918," *The Mariner's Mirror*, Vol. 100, No. 3, 2014; and Lawrence Sondhaus, *German Submarine Warfare in World War I: The Onset of Total War at Sea*, London: Rowman & Littlefield, 2017, among many possible sources.

[6]   See Chapter Two and Appendix A for details of oil and rubber interdiction efforts during WWII.

the physical destruction of the enemy's war materiel but also the diversion of resources from the main war effort and the imposition of costs by increasing trade-offs between military and nonmilitary imperatives.

Today, kinetic supply interdiction efforts still concern war planners: Blockades, piracy, and—a more recent addition to the interdiction repertoire—cyberattacks are stock strategies of modern warfare. But thanks to the speed, sophistication, and deep level of globalization of modern trade and financial markets, it is conceivable that the same effects that classic kinetic supply interdiction efforts seek to achieve could be induced instead, under the right conditions, by nonkinetic market dynamics. For instance, one could imagine any number of ill-timed events, from typhoons to trade policy changes to mergers and acquisitions, driving up a combatant's shipping and maritime insurance costs in the early months of a military conflict, as the *Emden* did.

What we refer to in this report as *economic shocks*—unanticipated changes in conditions of markets upon which combatant supplies and economies rely—could derive from innumerable sources. Irrespective of the trigger of an economic shock, a key assertion underlying this study is that the United States, its allies, and its adversaries might be differentially exposed to the damaging consequences of some shocks, so that economic shocks can impart asymmetric military advantage tantamount to the classic military strategy of supply interdiction.

The 2018 National Defense Strategy characterizes the global security environment as having reentered an era of peer and near-peer competition.[7] One characteristic distinguishing peer and near-peer countries is economic might: Achieving world-class military capability requires tremendous economic resources, the accumulation of which might essentially require substantial participation in global trade and finance. But, as widely accepted economic models suggest, countries enter international markets with distinct comparative advantages—different endowments of natural resources, human and physical capital, technology, and institutional capacities—which

---

[7] Department of Defense, *Summary of the 2018 National Defense Strategy of the United States of America*, Washington, D.C., 2018.

enable them to compete in world markets.[8] In effect, participation in global markets, and thus the potential to achieve peer or near-peer status, implies an internationally unique economic structure that renders countries' economies and defense industrial bases (DIBs) differentially exposed to disruption from economic shocks. The premise of this report is that under some circumstances, this differential exposure could conceivably result in asymmetric military advantage.

Against this backdrop, in early 2020, the Defense Advanced Research Projects Agency (DARPA) asked the RAND National Security Research Division (NSRD) to examine opportunities for better leveraging data analysis to support decisionmakers responsible for managing the risks that economic shocks pose to DIB capabilities.

This report discusses NSRD's research effort, which complements a body of other recent RAND work: Silberglitt et al., 2013, investigates the reliance of U.S. manufacturing on imported critical materials. Bond et al., 2020, reviews the economic consequences of hurricanes Irma and Maria in 2017 on Puerto Rico. Welburn and Strong, 2020, estimates the effects of coronavirus disease 2019 (COVID-19) on corporate default risk. Welburn et al., 2020, infers a firm-level network and subsequently estimates firm-level input-output (I-O) flows. Finally, at a more strategic level, Shatz and Chandler, 2020, considers the implications of global economic trends, including trade patterns, on the future of warfare.[9]

---

[8] A large body of literature explores the relationship between factor endowments and international trade patterns. Classic examples of such trade models include the Ricardian model of international trade, which is the first recorded exposition on comparative advantage, and the Heckscher-Ohlin model, which builds on the Ricardian model and proposes that a nation's factor endowments drive its comparative advantage in international trade. Traditional undergraduate-level international trade textbooks describe such models. For a fairly recent evaluation of the empirical evidence for Heckscher-Ohlin and alternative models, see Peter K. Schott, "One Size Fits All? Heckscher-Ohlin Specialization in Global Production," *American Economic Review*, Vol. 93, No. 3, 2003.

[9] Richard Silberglitt, James T. Bartis, Brian G. Chow, David L. An, and Kyle Brady, *Critical Materials: Present Danger to U.S. Manufacturing*, Santa Monica, Calif.: RAND Corporation, RR-133-NIC, 2013; Craig A. Bond, Aaron Strong, Troy D. Smith, Megan Andrew, John S. Crown, Kathryn A. Edwards, Gabriella C. Gonzalez, Italo A. Gutierrez, Lauren Kendrick, Jill E. Luoto, Kyle Pratt, Karishma V. Patel, Alexander D. Rothenberg, Mark Stalczynski, Patricia K. Tong, and Melanie A. Zaber, *Challenges and Opportuni-*

This report differs from existing research in both focus and scope. In terms of focus, this is the only report of which we are aware that examines supply interdiction effects as potentially being triggered by economic shocks. In terms of scope, at DARPA's request, we have kept a wide aperture to the types of economic shocks and DIB capabilities we consider. Consequently, this report does not rest on any assertions about which shocks, DIB capabilities, or military consequences matter. This scoping has the advantage of avoiding preconceived limitations on what dynamics drive outcomes. But it also presents a challenge, because it requires careful consideration of which dynamics might generalize to many shock instances and which might be specific only to some.

The Disruptive Potential of Economic Shocks

The generation and sustainment of DIB capability depends on the reliable flow of resources that constitute production inputs—raw materials, intermediate goods, facilities, tools and equipment, labor, technology, expertise, financial capital, etc.—through its production process, which often includes numerous tiers in a supply chain. Economic shocks are unanticipated changes—at any point in the production process—in the conditions on which resource allocation decisions are based. An economic shock might lead a decisionmaker somewhere in the supply chain or within the defense establishment itself to alter resource allocations. Such decisions might change conditions for decisionmakers elsewhere in the production process, which might change conditions for yet other decisionmakers, and so

ties for the Puerto Rico Economy: A Review of Evidence and Options Following Hurricanes Irma and Maria in 2017, Homeland Security Operational Analysis Center operated by the RAND Corporation, RR-2600-DHS, 2020; Jonathan Welburn and Aaron Strong, Estimating the Impact of COVID-19 on Corporate Default Risk, Santa Monica, Calif.: RAND Corporation, WR-A173-2, 2020; Jonathan Welburn, Aaron Strong, Florentine Eloundou Nekoul, Justin Grana, Krystyna Marcinek, Osonde A. Osoba, Nirabh Koirala, and Claude Messan Setodji, Systemic Risk in the Broad Economy: Interfirm Networks and Shocks in the U.S. Economy, Santa Monica, Calif.: RAND Corporation, RR-4185-RC, 2020; Howard J. Shatz and Nathan Chandler, Global Economic Trends and the Future of Warfare: The Changing Global Environment and Its Implications for the U.S. Air Force, Santa Monica, Calif.: RAND Corporation, RR-2849/4-AF, 2020.

on, risking a cascade of changes throughout the network of interconnected entities composing a supply chain, industry, market, or economy. Some changes in allocation decisions might result in *supply restrictions*, such as cost increases or even limited supply at any price.

As presented in more detail in Chapter Two, examples of events that might qualify as shocks include natural disasters, armed conflicts, epidemics, technological developments, regulatory changes, trade policy changes, the publication of business and economic data, and the announcement of a business merger. Table 1.1 lists examples of types of economic shocks organized into three categories: those derived primarily from market-based events, those derived from changes to government economic policy, and those derived from nonmarket events.[10] Whatever the cause of the shock, the defining feature is that it changes decisionmakers' evaluations of the factors on which resource allocation decisions are based, potentially leading to a change of allocation decisions.

Existing academic and policy research on economic shocks has not, to the best of our knowledge, systematically examined the effects of economic shocks on the generation of defense capability. Existing literature

TABLE 1.1

Examples of Types of Shocks

Market	Government Policy	Nonmarket
Commodity prices	Government spending	Technical innovation
Labor supply	Taxation policy	Natural disasters
Labor demand	Monetary policy	Cyberattacks
Financial events	Exchange rate policy	Wars
Risk premia	Trade policy	
Unpredictable human behavior and uncertainty	Regulatory and legal policy	
News and information		

---

[10] This not a comprehensive list of shocks or of categorizations. In fact, the shocks and categories might not even be mutually exclusive, because one shock can trigger another shock and the root cause of a cascade of shocks can be difficult to identify. Instead, this table provides examples of changes that this report addresses.

in economics tends to look at the effects of specific shocks on aggregate or sectoral-level economic activity as measured by, for example, gross domestic product (GDP) or unemployment (see Appendix B). In contrast, we aspire to advance a systems-level understanding of the factors determining whether, to what extent, and under what conditions various types of economic shocks degrade military capability or otherwise compromise defense postures.

Figure 1.1 depicts our conceptualization of the chain of events by which an economic shock might achieve the degradation of military capability through its effects on a DIB. On the left side of the figure in blue boxes are the DIB and its supply chains that produce a military capability (such as a weapon system) and provide inputs for its operations and sustainment. Typically, private-sector decisionmakers such as firm executives are most directly responsible for managing the effects of economic shocks on blue-box entities and dynamics. On the right side of the figure in green boxes are the military and other relevant governmental institutions that make decisions and operationalize the capability to achieve military effects. Typically, public-sector decisionmakers such as political and military leaders are most directly responsible for managing the effects of economic shocks on green-box entities and dynamics.

The main pathway by which we envision an economic shock disrupting this process is by changing the allocation decisions of an entity in the DIB or its supply chain—the blue box. For instance, a natural disaster might destroy an existing source of inputs, rendering that input unavailable in the

FIGURE 1.1

Key Points in a Notional Propagation Pathway of Economic Shocks to Military Capabilities

short run and increasing its price over a longer time horizon. Consequently, the DIB either might not be able to provide defense capability because it cannot obtain a required input or might only be able to provide the defense capability at a higher cost.

At several points in this chain of events, there might be processes or resources that can shield defense capability from degradation. Several notional points of such resilience are marked in green at the top of Figure 1.1. For instance, entities in the affected DIB or its supply chain might have stockpiled the disrupted input or might be able to pivot quickly to an alternative source. Military commanders or planners might be able to generate the disrupted weapon system's capabilities through alternative means. The defining aspect of resilience—which might most usefully be viewed as existing on a spectrum—is that it cushions the defense capability generation process from damage and costs caused by an economic shock: A more-resilient process suffers less-severe damage and cost increase (again, potentially measured in terms of trade-offs against other imperatives) from a shock than does a less-resilient system.[11]

The exact mechanisms by which shocks degrade the generation of a military capability through a DIB can be challenging to ascertain in many situations but are important for the policy considerations in this report. Table 1.2 lists several characteristics that we propose are central to the effects of a shock. Several of these characteristics describe a time dimension: *Latency* refers to the delay between when a shock occurs and when its effects are felt; *duration* refers to the interval of time over which a shock persists; and *variability* refers to the change in intensity of the shock over the shock duration. Time can also be an important consideration for the final two characteristics: *Reach* refers to the ripple or spillover effects of a shock. Markets, industries, supply chains, and economies are interconnected networks, so an event such as an economic shock that happens in one part of the net-

---

[11] Antifragility is not directly considered in this report, although many of the methods and constructs used to study resilience may be relevant to antifragility as well. Antifragility is a property describing a system that improves as a result of a shock, rather than simply withstanding or recovering from the shock. Sections of this report that discuss adaptation might be especially relevant to consideration of antifragility. For a nontechnical description of antifragility, see Nassim Nicholas Taleb, *Antifragile: Things That Gain from Disorder, Incerto Vol. 3*, New York: Random House, 2012.

TABLE 1.2

Taxonomy of Economic Shock Characteristics

Characteristic Type	Can or do events occur and unfold . . .
Latency	rapidly or gradually and potentially with delay?
Duration	in a fixed interval or indefinitely?
Variability	with intensity that changes over shock duration?
Reach	locally—e.g., within a contained market or geography—or across markets and, potentially, globally?
Visibility	with high or low observability?

SOURCE: Adapted from unpublished RAND research that identifies four characteristics of cyber incidents: onset (what this report calls *latency*), duration, visibility, and reach.

work can have effects in other parts of the network. *Visibility* encapsulates the features of a shock event that might render it detectable to the entities potentially affected by the shock. The reach and visibility of a shock might depend in part on time-related factors, such as time-related shock characteristics or the speed with which shocked entities respond and adapt to shock consequences.

We propose that the propagation of a shock and its effects on the generation of military capability do not depend solely on features of the shock itself but also on features of the DIB and on the success of entities in the production process in responding and adapting to the shock. Entities that might be affected by an economic shock can take actions to avoid it or to mitigate and recover from its disruptive effects. But such adaptation entails several substeps, which we represent by drawing upon the construct of the observe, orient, decide, act (OODA) loop used in a variety of applications, such as military command and control.[12, 13] Completing each step of the OODA

---

[12] Attributed to John Boyd. See, for instance, John R. Boyd, "The Essence of Winning and Losing," unpublished lecture notes, revised January 1996.

[13] In recent years, there has been ongoing discussion about whether the OODA loop or the more-recent act-sense-decide-adapt (ASDA) cycle is a more appropriate metaphor for modern warfare. The concepts in this report could be recast as ASDA cycles, for instance, by emphasizing the adaptive nature of complex systems, such as economies, DIBs, supply chains, and national security policy. We employ the longer-standing OODA loop metaphor for the purposes of this exploratory work, primarily because it is

loop takes resources and, perhaps most importantly for the purposes of this study, time.

In Chapter Four, we leverage a notional model whereby the consequences of an economic shock depend critically upon the outcome of a race between the shock's propagation and the response and adaptation processes of affected entities: The more the affected entities' OODA loops can stay "inside" of the occurrence and propagation of economic shocks (that is, the faster potentially affected entities can detect and appropriately respond to the particular shock), the less damage suffered. In this model, depicted in Figure 1.2, DIB production process characteristics, such as production time and supply chain structure, mediate the speed of both shock propagation and entity response and adaptation. The model partitions shock events into three categories for subsequent analysis: Short-latency shocks can potentially affect ongoing combat operations; long-latency shocks are most relevant in long-term competition, affecting production capabilities and technology; and, finally, an intermediate latency period exists between these two extremes. We suspect that the outcome of the race between shock propagation and response and adaptation is most "competitive" for intermediate-latency shocks in the sense that the extent to which shock effects outpace response outcomes is most sensitive to variation in the production process characteristics, such as those identified in Figure 1.2. Viewed through the lens of this model, managing the effects of economic shocks on the generation of DIB capability is facilitated by an understanding of the sensitivity of shock propagation and response speed outcomes to system characteristics and the development of tools for influencing those pivotal sets of characteristics.

---

more widely known, and secondarily because our focus was most directly on topics that are well described by the "orientation" step of the OODA loop. For more information on OODA versus ASDA, see Justin Kelly and Mike Brennan, "OODA Versus ASDA: Metaphors at War," *Australian Army Journal*, Vol. VI, No. 3, Summer 2009.

FIGURE 1.2

Time-Oriented Model of Shock Features Versus Adaptation of the Shocked Entity

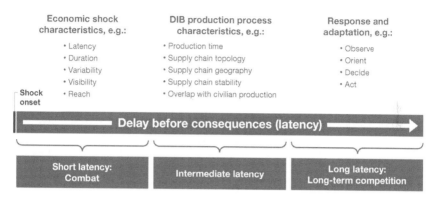

Economic shock characteristics, e.g.:	DIB production process characteristics, e.g.:	Response and adaptation, e.g.:
• Latency	• Production time	• Observe
• Duration	• Supply chain topology	• Orient
• Variability	• Supply chain geography	• Decide
• Visibility	• Supply chain stability	• Act
Shock onset • Reach	• Overlap with civilian production	

Delay before consequences (latency)

Short latency: Combat	Intermediate latency	Long latency: Long-term competition

Advancing Methodologies for Analyzing Economic Shocks

The conceptual models summarized earlier suggest a variety of questions that an analytic toolkit would ideally help to address: To which types of economic shocks are various DIB capabilities most exposed? Under what conditions might economic shocks disrupt DIB capability generation by compromising access to market-based resources, such as traded commodities and components, intellectual property, or capital? By what mechanisms do economic shocks propagate through supply chains? What factors drive the speed of shock propagation? What are the consequences of these shocks for collateral markets—that is, how do shocks spill over to other markets? What characteristics of defense systems and capabilities, DIBs, firms, industries, markets, economies, and adaptation and response OODA loops drive resilience to shocks?

Answering these questions is difficult because, as we discuss in more detail in Chapter Two, there are several technical obstacles to measuring shocks and their effects. DARPA asked the RAND analysis team to assess the extent to which modern empirical methods from economics overcome those technical obstacles and then, in light of those findings, to lay out a path to improving U.S. Department of Defense (DoD) capabilities for leveraging data analysis to better support decisionmakers responsible for managing the defense implications of economic shocks. A substantial body of economics literature on shocks has grappled with many of the above-mentioned challenges with some success, developing empirical methodologies suitable for a wide range of circumstances of interest to the economics community. In this report, we examine the extent to which these methodologies satisfy the analytic needs of defense decisionmakers.

The objective of this report is to take initial steps toward building a DoD capability to analyze economic shocks. There are two desired outputs of this report. First, this report provides an impression of the extent to which further investment in developing such a capability is called for and is feasible. This report does not offer a comprehensive and quantitative benefit cost analysis of such an effort. Instead, it provides qualitative impressions and identifies considerations that a more-formal benefit cost analysis might take into account. Second, this report offers a broad outline of an approach to achieving such a capability, as well as some initial foundational work upon which future efforts could build. One of our recommendations is that DoD should invest in a larger effort to develop analytic support to decisionmakers responsible for managing the defense consequences of economic shocks. We hope that this report provides a helpful starting point in such an effort by making progress on an important first step: defining and structuring the problem.

Research Approach

Given the novelty of the risk environment that DARPA envisioned, a primary requirement of this research is to delineate the contours of that new environment. Following the model of the Heilmeier Catechism, developed by former DARPA director George H. Heilmeier to evaluate the merits of proposed DARPA programs,[14] we framed the analysis by focusing on several core questions:

---

[14] Heilmeier developed a dialectic approach to help proposers think through and evaluate the merit of agency research under consideration. Core elements of the catechism included such questions as "What are you trying to achieve?" "How is the task done

- What are the questions of interest that defense decisionmakers need addressed to manage the effects of economic shocks on DIBs?
- What are today's workhorse methods for modeling the effects of these shocks?
- What are the challenges to addressing the questions of interest with existing methods and approaches?
- What would a new approach look like, and how could a new DARPA program help to improve capability?

To achieve these interrelated objectives, the research employed several lines of effort.

Exploration of Historical and Hypothetical Vignettes

An early step in our exploration of the potential value of improved DoD analytic capability was understanding the potential consequences of shocks on defense postures, what management options defense decisionmakers might consider, and what contextual factors might drive the feasibility of options. For this, we primarily looked to history. We engaged with subject-matter experts (SMEs) in defense acquisitions and DIB challenges and asked them about instances in which economic shocks—or kinetic actions whose market effects could also be triggered by economic shocks—had military consequences. One limitation of relying on historical instances is that it excludes scenarios enabled by exclusively modern conditions. To compensate for this limitation, we also asked a SME to develop a hypothetical scenario drawing on current geopolitical and economic conditions.

The outcome of this process was a series of vignettes describing each shock instance, including pertinent contextual information such as economic, political, or military conditions surrounding the instance; actions taken in response to the shock; and shock consequences. The vignettes helped us to understand why we might care about shocks and what sorts of questions a capability to analyze shocks would ideally be able to address.

today and why might it not work in the future?" "What is new in your approach and what are its risks?" and "How would you evaluate success?" See DARPA, "The Heilmeier Catechism," undated.

Altogether, analyzing vignettes served as a shaping exercise that helped the research team to focus on a concrete set of decisions and contextual factors that a data-informed analytic capability should account for. We refer to the desirable features of an analytic capability as *analytic capability requirements*.

In addition to establishing objectives for an analytic capability, examination of the vignettes led the research team to several preliminary modeling approaches that subsequent research efforts might consider incorporating. For instance, examination of the responses of entities affected by the shocks inspired the problem formulation captured in Figure 1.2, in which the effects of an economic shock depend in part on the response and adaptation capabilities of the potentially affected entities. Also, several of the vignettes feature situations in which we hypothesize that the effects of a shock depend on the recent history of prior shocks, which implies that a time series modeling approach might be appropriate in some situations.

Review of Economics Literature on Shocks

The next step was to examine current capabilities. We pursued this by reviewing the economics literature on shocks. We focused our review on how this literature defines, classifies, and empirically identifies shocks; outcomes studied in the literature; and—especially—the empirical methods that researchers use to study how shocks affect the outcomes of interest. A notable finding from this literature review, detailed in Appendix A, is that a relatively modest portfolio of four empirical methods (what we call *workhorse methods*) are widely used across a wide range of shocks and outcomes of interest in the economics literature.

These methods are not necessarily in competition which each other. Instead, they each offer a different type of insight into the consequences of a shock. For instance, one of the workhorse methods, vector autoregression (VAR), is helpful for tracking the consequences of a shock over a long period of time. In contrast, I-O analyses are helpful for examining the short-run spillover effects that a shock in one market might have in other markets. In isolation, each of the workhorse methods examines specific and different analytic questions about the effects of a shock. In combination, they help paint a more comprehensive picture of the consequences of an economic shock. However, there are limitations on the circumstances in which each method can be employed, and there are conditions under which their results might be inaccurate or imprecise. One objective of our literature review was to survey the conditions under which each method can be used and the factors affecting the accuracy and precision of the results that each method provides.

Gap Analysis

Our next line of effort was examining gaps between the analytic capability requirements suggested by the vignettes and the capabilities provided by existing empirical methods from economics, with particular focus on the four workhorse methods. Our analysis of vignettes yielded three core management challenges—which we call *management foci*—that shocks pose to defense decisionmakers: supply restrictions, potential inference of government priorities, and risk of extreme response to a shock. In the gap analysis, we examined the extent to which existing empirical methods from economics can inform these management foci.

To discipline this gap analysis, we proposed several analytic questions that an ideal empirical analysis would be able to answer in order to provide each analytic capability requirement, and then we examined the extent to which the workhorse methods answer the analytic questions. For example, one analytic capability requirement for analyzing the risk of extreme response to a shock is estimating the probability that a shock will lead to an extreme response. One analytic question whose answers would help provide this capability is the following: How will the shock affect key macroeconomic indicators, key economic sectors, and key political constituencies? Our research suggests that, given sufficient data, existing empirical methods from economics are well suited to answering the first two parts of this question but are probably less useful for answering the last without supplemental analytic approaches.

Output of the gap analysis contributes to the recommendations presented in the report's concluding chapter, which describes steps that DARPA or other defense agencies could take to advance methods for informing decisions central to managing the effects of economic shocks on DIBs.

Preliminary Development of a Framework for Shock-Induced Supply Disruptions

The gap analysis identifies potential benefits of developing *frameworks*—application and context-specific suites of models of key mechanisms driving shock occurrence, propagation, and consequences. Frameworks impart value primarily by connecting analytic outputs to the alternative courses of action (COAs) for managing shock consequences.

We envision frameworks as consisting of several modules, each of which illuminates a particular mechanism relevant to the decisionmaker's choice between alternative COAs. For instance, to help decisionmakers choose between alternative means of protecting defense supply chains from a shock, a framework might incorporate one module examining the near-term consequences of each COA, while another module might examine the long-term consequences of each COA. Or there might be different modules to examine different outcomes of interest. Different mechanisms might drive COA consequences for these different time horizons and outcomes, and, therefore, different analytic approaches might be needed. Modules might also form a hierarchy, with some modules providing integration of analysis with decisionmaking and other modules focusing on specific components of the analysis. The exact composition of a framework will vary from one situation to the next, depending on context-specific factors, such as the nature of the economic shock, consequences of concern, COAs under consideration, and the economic and political institutions in the markets of interest. Frameworks help to identify what analytic approaches to employ and then stitch the results of all analyses into a single coherent operating picture for decisionmakers.

In Chapter Four, we present a preliminary framework to support management of shock-induced supply disruptions. This framework consists of a hierarchy of modules. A high-level module provides a heuristic for selecting relevant lower-level modules based on contextual features, such as shock latency. Lower-level modules draw on empirical and theoretical methods across a range of disciplines—including economics, political science, and sociology—to leverage available data to inform decisionmaking.

Case Study

Our final research line of effort was to simulate a decisionmaking environment that captures many of the essential features of the vignettes and to
apply the workhorse empirical economics methods to inform policy questions in this environment. The objective of this case study was to further
explore the envisioned decisionmaking support analytic capability by identifying the range of questions that a methodology would ideally inform and
to achieve a more-precise, practically informed understanding of the potential and limits of existing empirical methods from economics.

Organization of This Report

In the next chapters, we discuss these research lines of effort further, concluding with a discussion of how our research findings suggest that existing
methodologies in economics could be leveraged to better support defense
decisionmakers. The remainder of this report is organized as follows:

Chapter Two provides a conceptual overview of the challenge of measuring the effects of economic shocks in the DIB. Through the introduction
of a set of vignettes, we highlight the features of interest in a future economic modeling capability to better capture those measurements.

Chapter Three introduces an array of existing methodological
approaches that can help capture the effects of shocks in an economy. This
survey not only addresses existing methods and their capabilities, but it also
provides an overview of technical challenges and potential gaps in the capability suite that senior leadership and stakeholders will find valuable.

Chapter Four expands on the concept of a framework as a decision support tool that can help close the capability gaps identified in Chapter Three.
This chapter presents a partial and preliminary framework for shock-
induced supply restriction.

Chapter Five advances the discussion in Chapters Three and Four
through an in-depth look at a quantitative case study. Here, the analysis
focuses on the case of repeated sanctions against Iran as an example of coor-
dinated, punitive economic shocks against a state intended to drive certain
behaviors in its DIB.

Chapter Six synthesizes the findings of the research lines of effort and proposes a path forward for economic modeling techniques. Here, the discussion offers a vision for a desired modeling capability, a synopsis of where today's methods currently stand in offering that capability, and the steps that might be required to arrive at an end state that would be more capable of capturing the effects of economic shocks. This concluding chapter offers two recommendations for how DoD might proceed to advance its economic modeling capabilities.

Appendixes A–C provide additional details on the review of economics literature on shocks, the vignettes, and the case study.

CHAPTER TWO

Analytic Capability Requirements for Supporting Management of the Defense Implication of Economic Shocks

The premise of this project is that unexpected economic events—economic shocks—have the potential to disrupt military capabilities through their effects on DIBs. In this chapter, we offer a technical definition of economic shocks that is based on how shocks might affect production decisions. Then we explore several vignettes: historical and hypothetical scenarios illustrating the threats that shocks pose to the generation of military capability. Finally, we analyze the vignettes to characterize the challenges and opportunities posed by economic shocks. The primary output of this chapter is a preliminary set of analytic capability requirements: If DoD desires a sophisticated capability to empirically analyze economic shocks, what do the vignettes suggest that capability should include? As we turn to evaluating the value of existing empirical tools in the next chapter, we will continue to draw on insights from the vignettes for inspiration and guidance.

What Are Economic Shocks?

For the purpose of this report, *economic shocks* are changes in the conditions upon which resource allocation decisions are based that are (1) unanticipated and (2) triggered by events outside the control of at least some decisionmakers in the DIB or defense decisionmaking establishment.[1] The inputs (land, labor, physical and financial capital, and technology) into the production of any good or service *could* have been used for other purposes. Some decisionmaking process—perhaps market based or perhaps political—directed inputs to the creation of the weapon system instead of something else. This type of allocation decision occurs at every level in a weapon system supply chain, since even for relatively simple goods and services, there are several distinct steps in the production process.

In deciding how to allocate scarce resources, decisionmakers face a difficult question of what the most valuable use of an input is. This will depend on a comparison of value across different potential uses of the input. In many cases, relative value depends on factors that are uncertain, often because the value depends on how things play out in the future. If something causes decisionmakers to change their calculation of the relative values of alternative uses for inputs or their calculation of the uncertainty of risk of relative valuations, those decisionmakers might alter their use of that input.[2]

Here are some specific notional examples of shocks and how they affect resource allocation:

- Policy: A tariff rate change makes a key input more expensive, and firms in the supply chain raise their prices for the defense prime contractor. The defense prime contractor then reduces its research and development (R&D) budget to absorb the cost increase.

---

[1] The material from this section represents a synthesis of descriptions of shocks in the economics literature. See Appendix B for more detail.

[2] An event that causes a decisionmaker to recalculate the relative value of alternative uses of an input might cause the decisionmaker to actually change their use of an input. However, the decisionmaker might instead choose to maintain the same use of that input, but then the true cost of that input will have changed, so allocations elsewhere in the economy must also change (unless there was a change in total resource availability). For example, if a shock causes an input's alternative use to increase in value, a decisionmaker might choose to not alter input use. But in this case, the implied cost of that allocation increases because the alternative use has higher value than it did before. In a market-based system, some change might result in a price increase, but even where costs are not fully measured by price, the fact remains that more is given up to achieve a particular allocation. Another way of saying this is that the opportunity cost of the choice made, or the value of foregone alternatives, increases.

- Nonmarket: Tech advancement leads a firm to change a product's configuration to please civilian customers. The firm then stops producing the legacy military-specific configuration to redirect resources to the more-profitable civilian market.
- Market: Booming wages in the natural gas industry attract workers who would otherwise have filled manufacturing jobs, putting upward pressure on domestic manufacturing labor costs and reducing domestic production capacity.
- Market: A specialty steel producer acquires its largest rival and stops small-batch production runs, instead limiting production to times when total market volume allows for the most economical production. Defense industries requiring this steel then fall behind schedule.

Vignettes

We engaged with SMEs on defense acquisitions and DIB challenges and asked them about instances in which economic shocks—or kinetic actions whose market effects could also be triggered by economic shocks—had military consequences. We supplemented these discussions with reviews of literature on the instances to which the SMEs pointed us. We also asked a SME to develop a hypothetical scenario drawing on current geopolitical and economic conditions. Table 2.1 summarizes the vignettes we analyzed. We provide brief descriptions of vignettes in this chapter, and Appendix B includes more details, as well as references.

Selecting vignettes by surveying SMEs imposes important limitations. We asked SMEs to provide us with historical examples of shocks so that we could explore modeling constructs with the benefit of knowing how shocks would play out. This effort is too preliminary to permit a full historical survey. The cost of our limited scope is that it risks imparting selection bias, so findings cannot be taken as representative of the entire range of possible relevant scenarios. An important example of selection bias is that this process excludes analysis of instances in which resilience prevented shocks from having adverse effects (the "dog that didn't bark" effect). On the other hand, to the extent that the vignettes are taken as evidence of the importance of economic shocks, this process risks overstating the expected risk of

TABLE 2.1

Summary of Vignettes

Vignettes	Summary[a]
Confederate industrial and financial constraints (U.S. Civil War, 1861–1865)	A U.S. embargo on trade and access to financial resources forced the Confederacy to quickly establish its own limited industry and financial system
U.S. rubber supply (WWII, 1939–1945)	Japan used military force to cut off Allied access to rubber, a key DIB input
German oil supply (WWII, 1939–1945)	Allied powers used economic and kinetic means to block Axis access to oil, degrading their DIB capability
British Shipbuilding (1977–1987)	Multiple abrupt changes in British industrial policy exacerbated ongoing production capability degradation
Iraq's invasion of Kuwait (1990)	Iraq invaded Kuwait, in the heart of the world's major oil-supplying region, after Kuwait refused to accede to Iraqi demands to alleviate the burden of Iraq's debts from the Iran-Iraq war
Cornered markets—i.e., critical materials (circa 2010)	Chinese industrial policy led to dominance of critical material extraction and processing capability, rendering countries such as the United States and Japan vulnerable to shocks from market manipulation and Chinese national policy
U.S. sanctions on Iran (2011–2020)	U.S. sanctions were intended to achieve specific objectives but introduced the risk of failure, collateral economic damage, and extreme response
U.S. Budget Control Act (2013)	The Government Accountability Office (GAO) found that budget cuts in 2013 adversely affected readiness and delayed acquisition programs; these cuts might have affected DIB structure
U.S. access to Russian RD-180 engines (circa 2014)	U.S. sanctions on Russia in response to the Ukraine crisis threatened U.S. access to space launch capability
Effects of energy price drop on Russia (2014–2016)	Oil and gas price reductions forced the Russian government to reduce spending, including weapon system development and production
COVID-19 DIB disruptions—e.g., Australian shipbuilding (2020)	The pandemic has delayed several defense programs, such as Australia's frigate and submarine programs
Hypothetical mobilization scenario	Asymmetry across countries in DIB structure and functioning means that economic shocks during mobilization could drive military advantage

[a] See text and Appendix B for details on and references for all vignettes with the exceptions of U.S. sanctions on Iran, which are detailed in Chapter Four, and the hypothetical mobilization vignette, which is fully detailed in this chapter.

damage from shocks, because we specifically focused on instances that had meaningful consequences.

Despite this limitation, the analysis here acts as an informative shaping exercise—namely, to serve as a survey for advancing understanding of potential effects of shocks on a nation's DIB and to move toward a systematic method for understanding, detecting, evaluating, and responding to such shocks. We derived from the vignettes a concrete set of analytic capability requirements that we used in Chapter Three as a benchmark against which to assess the value of existing empirical methods from economics.

Confederate Industrial and Financial Constraints During the U.S. Civil War (1861–1865)

After the battle of Fort Sumter in April 1861, the Confederate States were suddenly cut off from the industrial and financial resources of the Union, leaving them unprepared for a protracted war. The Confederate Ordnance Department—the organization charged with supplying Confederate forces with arms and munitions—eventually established sources of supply that met, although unsustainably at the conflict's end, the Confederate military's demand for the tools of war. However, the Confederacy was unable to generate sufficient revenue through taxes, bonds, or loans, nor was it able to coordinate transportation demands across the South. The Confederacy tried to meet near-term fiscal demands by printing fiat currency, but the large increase in the money supply soon led to a vicious cycle of increasing prices and hoarding of essential commodities by private businesses. By 1864, the inflation-induced shortages, exacerbated by degraded transportation networks across the South, left both soldiers and civilians malnourished, underdressed, underpaid, and with low morale. With labor stretched thin among agriculture, industry, and the front lines; supply chains dismantled by Union forces or poor management; and an ineffective financial system, the Confederacy could no longer sustain its war effort or the government itself.

Contested U.S. Rubber Supply in World War II (1939–1945)

Prior to its entry into WWII, the United States received almost the entirety of its rubber supply from British Malaya and the Netherlands East Indies, which together produced 90 percent of the world's natural rubber. In 1942, Japanese forces cut off U.S. access to the natural rubber supply being harvested from these regions. At the time, rubber was a critical material in many U.S. military supply chains. Not only was rubber essential in the production of common spares, such as tires, but it was also an essential component of electrical wiring to provide insulation. As early as 1934, U.S. government officials recognized the U.S.'s dependency on the few rubber-producing islands, as well as their vulnerability to Japanese encroachment in the region. However, due to the Roosevelt administration's hesitation to fund stockpiling initiatives preceding and during the 1937–1938 recession to avoid spending deficits, the U.S. government did not authorize widespread stockpiling until 1939, and it dramatically increased investment in the development of alternative sources of rubber—such as large-scale processes for producing synthetic rubber—after U.S. entry into the war in December 1941. Albeit rushed, these efforts—and especially a 200-fold increase in synthetic rubber production in the period from 1939–1945—provided sufficient rubber to fully meet all military needs. However, fulfilling military requirements (which were often overstated) also came at the cost of reductions in civilian consumption.

Disruptions to Germany's Oil Access During World War II (1939–1945)

Prior to WWII, Germany relied on imports for 70 percent of its annual oil supply—the vast majority of which came from overseas. German officials recognized the vulnerability of these imports in event of war and began investing in a self-sufficient, domestic oil industry—centered on synthetic oil production—as soon as the Nazi government took power in 1933. As anticipated, once the war began, Germany lost access to overseas imports and shortly thereafter lost access to oil from Russia, Germany's second largest supplier on the continent. With its burgeoning domestic industry, along with severe cuts to civilian consumption and efforts by the German military to ration its limited supply, Germany managed to persist despite these shocks and even saw record oil supplies by early 1944. Although Germany's access to oil was not critical before 1944, the shocks here nonetheless degraded military effectiveness, most notably by restricting pilot training hours and further motorization of the German army.

In May 1944, the Allied bombing campaign, combined with the Soviet capture of Nazi production sites, such as those in Romania, began delivering the fatal shock to the German oil industry, reducing production to just 12 percent of its peak by March 1945. Aviation fuel supply quickly dwindled, grounding most of the Luftwaffe's record number of aircraft within months. Fuel consumption for ground forces persisted until stocks were depleted in September and then were cut drastically thereafter, leaving German field officers unable to make proper tactical use of their equipment.

Nationalization and Reprivatization Disrupt Ownership and Management of the British Shipbuilding Industrial Base (1977–1987)

Throughout the 1970s and 1980s, shipbuilding was one of many British industries and manufactories caught up in the changing directions of the larger political-economic environment. Under government by the Labour Party in the mid-1960s to the late 1970s, the industry was nationalized, meaning that swathes of the industry were brought under the banner of a state-owned enterprise, British Shipbuilding. After the election of the Conservative Party government headed by Margaret Thatcher in 1979, many state-owned companies were lined up to be sold back to the private sector. British Shipbuilding's turn to do so came in 1988.

Amid these to-and-fro domestic political forces, the UK's shipbuilding industry was facing significant global headwinds. East Asian countries such as Japan and Korea were manufacturing and exporting cheaper ships. Meanwhile, longer-term changes in commercial shipping patterns had resulted from the oil crises of the 1970s. Finally, the onset of the jet age led to the sunset of all but the last remnants of the transatlantic passenger shipping business. Contemporary reports state that public ownership caused shuffling of orders around shipyards because of political considerations, while privatization's installation of new management staff caused disorder and delays. Such outcomes had the potential to compromise the ability of the shipbuilding industrial base to deliver naval assets that met quality and timeline requirements.

Iraqi Invasion of Kuwait (1990)

The nearly decade-long Iran-Iraq war left the Iraqi government facing war debt, reconstruction costs, and domestic demands that it could not afford with its annual revenues, 95 percent of which were based on oil exports. In response, Iraq's president, Saddam Hussein, demanded that Kuwait and other Gulf nations provide Iraq with capital, forgive their wartime debts, and reduce their own oil production quotas so that Iraq could increase production without depressing prices—demands that Iraq justified as repayment for defending the Arab nations from Iranian expansion. Kuwait refused. To Iraq, Kuwait was unjustly waging economic war.

On August 2, 1990, Iraqi forces invaded Kuwait. From the Iraqi perspective, forcibly appropriating Kuwait's resources would allow Iraq to afford reconstruction efforts, meet domestic demands, and repay its debts within five years. Denouncing the invasion, the United Nations (UN) swiftly applied sanctions, and by December, Iraq was reported to have lost 90 percent of its imports and 97 percent of its exports. Coalition military efforts soon struck valuable targets in Iraq, further constraining the economy, and eventually removed Iraqi forces from Kuwait. The sanctions and effects of the Gulf War left conditions in Iraq, described at one point as a return to the 19th century, below preinvasion levels for years to come. From the U.S. perspective, the Iraqi invasion of Kuwait and the ensuing Gulf War cost the United States approximately $100 billion in 2011 dollars and 147 combat deaths and aggravated the ongoing recession with a spike in oil prices and increased economic uncertainty.

Cornered Markets: China Changed Its Rare Earth Materials Export Controls to Limit Japanese Access During a Diplomatic Dispute (2010)

China's dominance of the extraction and processing of critical rare earth materials left Japan vulnerable to the economic shock of export controls. China currently dominates world markets, both in extraction and processing, for certain rare earth materials that are small but crucial inputs in manufactured systems. In 2010, a collision between Chinese and Japanese vessels in disputed waters near the Senkaku Islands escalated into a diplomatic crisis, with one manifestation being an embargo of rare earth materials exports from China to Japan. Chinese officials implicitly implemented the embargo by delaying export and customs control certificates for shipments of rare earth elements that were ready to be shipped to Japan, rather than creating an explicit new trade policy. Although the matter was resolved in a matter of weeks, the potent implications of rare earth materials as a political-economic bargaining chip were made apparent. A persistent disruption could have caused crippling delays and shortages in Japan's electronics industry.

U.S. Sanctions on Iran (2011–2020)

As we discuss in further detail in Chapter Four, a recent form of an intentional economic shock was the imposition of sanctions on Iran by the United States. The United States has levied various sanctions against Iran since 1979. A primary objective of recent rounds of sanctions has been to delay Iran's achievement of nuclear weapon capability. We focus on the effects of sanctions that have occurred in a number of waves since the 2015 Joint Comprehensive Plan of Action (JCPOA). Although sanctions have been applied to numerous sectors (e.g., energy, shipping, banking, construction, mining, textiles, manufacturing, and metals), they have historically focused on the oil industry, which is a significant driver of the Iranian economy.

U.S. Budget Control Act of 2013

In 2013, the U.S. Congress failed to reach an agreement on alternative budget cuts, thus triggering what became known as the budget sequestration. For months before the Budget Control Act was passed, until around midnight on the day that the Budget Control Act went into effect, Congress attempted to negotiate alternative budget cuts. Uncertainty around the magnitude and allocation of budget cuts, as well as the ultimate change in spending, constituted an economic shock that changed the conditions underlying the allocation decisions of defense contractors and their supply chains, as well as defense workers and their households. In terms of documented concrete consequences for defense capabilities, GAO found that furloughs in contracting and acquisition offices harmed readiness and caused delays in acquisition programs.

Sanctions Against Russia Force the United States to Initiate an Acquisition Program to Replace RD-180 Rocket Engines (2014)

Russian actions annexing Crimea in 2014 prompted a response by the U.S. Congress that included a package of economic sanctions. Congress was concerned that the targets of the sanctions could continue to profit from or influence the United States via purchases of Russian-made RD-180 rocket engines and thus sought to restrict their import. These engines power the Atlas V launch vehicle, which is regularly used for space-related missions. As of 2014, there was no viable alternative to power the Atlas V, meaning that a ban on imports of RD-180 engines would have left the United States with a finite existing supply. Originally, Congress intended for the RD-180 to be phased out by 2019. Due to schedule slippage in the development of domestic replacements, the RD-180 is expected to be used until at least 2022. The RD-180 engine technology is cheap and reliable, making it a staple of national security and defense space launch missions. As the United States aerospace industry attempts to manufacture a replacement, there is no guarantee that it will be able to replicate all the desirable technical features.

The Effects of Energy Price Shocks on Russian Government Spending (2014–2016)

In 2014, almost half of Russia's federal budget was funded by oil and gas revenues. Between 2014 and 2016, drops in the price of oil took a toll on Russia's economic resources, reducing state revenues by a quarter. Overall, this led to an approximate 15 percent decline in the Russian federal budget by 2016. This presented a challenging resource allocation problem for Russian leadership. Russia ultimately decided to utilize its Reserve Fund to continue armament production. As the fund's balance neared zero, production continued at a lower rate and with prioritization for key weapon systems.

COVID-19 Lockdowns for Foreign Contractors Delay Australian Naval Acquisitions (2020)

The COVID-19 pandemic unfolded as an exogenous disruption affecting every national DIB across the globe. Australia's DIB faced a challenge qualitatively different from many others. Its defense acquisition depended on foreign suppliers that were under completely different lockdown regimes. Specifically, the Australian Navy's submarine and frigate acquisition programs faced schedule slippage risk due to British and French government restrictions preventing design contractors there from working on the Australian projects.

The Possibility of an Economic Shock Coinciding with International Military Mobilization (Hypothetical Scenario)

As discussed in Chapter One, a premise underlying this study is the possibility that countries might be differentially affected by an economic shock to a globalized market. This vignette focuses on a hypothetical scenario in which differences in shock consequences across countries could prove militarily decisive. In particular, the vignette envisions a baseline scenario in which an economic shock hits a market on which the world's major militaries rely to build or sustain important weapon systems. Moreover, the shock hits while countries are already in the midst of a military buildup or mobilization.[3]

Under such conditions, the economic shock could impart an asymmetric advantage to those countries that either are less exposed to the shock or that pivot most quickly to effectively mitigate the effects of the shock. A country might be relatively less exposed to the shock if its weapon systems rely less on the shocked global market, perhaps due to different technological underpinnings. A country might also be relatively less exposed if its mil-

---

[3] None of these scenarios is intended to predict future events. Instead, the purpose of this vignette and its variations is to consider a range of conditions under which global economic shocks could coincide with mobilization in a way that favors the military objectives of some countries.

itary doctrine is less dependent than other nations on the weapon systems affected by the shock.

Several factors might affect the relative speed with which a country responds to the shock. For instance, a country's economic structure, along with the economic structures of its allies and nonadversarial trading partners, might drive response speed. Some economic structures might accommodate faster *mobilization*, or recruitment of civilian production inputs for military purposes. Similarly, a country's political institutions related to the authorization and funding of military expenditures might also play an important role. Countries may vary in the extent of political support for mobilization or in institutional decisionmaking speed.

This hypothetical scenario could apply to many different groups of potential ally and adversarial groups throughout the world. Aside from a scenario involving China, Russia, the United States, and major U.S. allies, scenarios involving large and growing countries, such as Brazil and India, also hold interesting lessons, since these countries have different economic and political structures.

The historical precedence of China's continuing military buildup since the 1990s[4,5,6] inspires some interesting variations of this hypothetical scenario. For instance, given the geographic concentration and limited capacity of the world's shipbuilding industry and supporting supply chains, a significant increase in China's buildup of naval forces could trigger its own economic shock. China might have an advantage over many of its adversaries if its own military shipbuilding activities disrupt related global markets, since China has a large commercial shipbuilding capacity. An alternative variation of this scenario reverses the causality: The economic shock of a

---

4 Office of the Secretary of Defense, *Military and Security Developments Involving the People's Republic of China 2020*, Washington, D.C., September 2020.

5 Eric Heginbotham, Michael Nixon, Forrest E. Morgan, Jacob L. Heim, Jeff Hagen, Sheng Tao Li, Jeffrey Engstrom, Martin C. Libicki, Paul DeLuca, David A. Shlapak, David R. Frelinger, Burgess Laird, Kyle Brady, and Lyle J. Morris, *The U.S.-China Military Scorecard: Forces, Geography, and the Evolving Balance of Power, 1996–2017*, Santa Monica, Calif.: RAND Corporation, RR-392-AF, 2015.

6 David A. Shlapak, David T. Orletsky, Toy I. Reid, Murray Scot Tanner, and Barry Wilson, *A Question of Balance: Political Context and Military Aspects of the China-Taiwan Dispute*, Santa Monica, Calif.: RAND Corporation, MG-888-SRF, 2009.

global downturn in demand for ships could produce surplus capacity in the Chinese shipbuilding industry that is utilized for a buildup.

Analysis of Vignettes

Next, we look for patterns to understand what these vignettes might indicate about the modern risk of economic shocks and how empirical analysis could contribute to management of those risks. Given the limitations imposed by the process by which we selected the vignettes, we intend the results of this analysis to serve as a starting point for developing an analytic capability. This report presents hypotheses, derived from our analysis of the vignettes, about the mechanisms by which economic shocks affect defense postures, such as the generation of military capability.

Our analysis leads to two findings:

- **Finding 1:** Economic shocks seem to have the potential to cause meaningful damage to defense postures.
- **Finding 2:** A modest portfolio of analytic capabilities would support management of a wide range of concerns about economic shocks.

Finding 1: Economic Shocks Seem to Have the Potential to Cause Meaningful Damage to Defense Postures

The first question we asked in analyzing our vignettes was whether there is indication that economic shocks pose risks to defense postures that are sufficiently meaningful to justify investment in improved analytic capability.[7] The ten vignettes listed in Table 2.2 demonstrate the potential for economic shocks to degrade military capability.[8]

---

[7] As mentioned in Chapter One, we cannot speak to a formal cost-benefit analysis, and we acknowledge that the vignettes suffer from selection bias. Consequently, this is not a formal evaluation; it is simply an exploratory effort to gauge the potential for damage and prospects for mitigation.

[8] Because the historical references we examined for the two remaining shocks, the Iraqi invasion of Kuwait (1990) and U.S. sanctions on Iran (2011–2020), did not provide clear evidence of actual or potential military damage, we excluded them from this

Kinetic Interdiction as Evidence of the Potential Consequences of Economic Shocks

The first three vignettes in Table 2.2, Confederate industrial and financial constraints (U.S. Civil War), the U.S. rubber supply (WWII), and the German oil supply (WWII), provide indirect evidence of the potentially meaningful military consequences of economic shocks. The "shock" underlying each of these vignettes is not actually an economic shock but a kinetic supply interdiction effort. We include these vignettes despite the absence of an instigating economic shock because we suspect that economic shocks could have similar effects.

The damage suffered by the Confederacy during the U.S. Civil War was derived from the fact that the Confederate industrial supply chains and financial systems depended on Union industry and financial infrastructure. When the Confederacy went to war with the Union, it lost access to these sources of supply. Likewise, rubber and oil production were geographically concentrated during the WWII era. Kinetic interdiction efforts were damaging in these situations because production was geographically concentrated and exposed to adversary influence. Nonkinetic adversary actions could similarly restrict access to war materiel with such production markets by leveraging political or economic influence—for instance, by restrictive trade policy or outbidding opponents for such materiel.

If economic shocks could have the same consequences on supply chains as these kinetic interdiction efforts, then economic shocks have the potential to cause similarly meaningful damage to defense postures.

Evidence of Supply Restriction

Two of the vignettes instigated by adversary kinetic actions, Confederate industrial and financial constraints (U.S. Civil War) and the German oil supply (WWII), demonstrate that supply restriction can severely compromise military operations by denying combatants access to materiel needed to prosecute operations. Insufficient access to food, clothing, and industrial goods directly contributed to the Confederacy's inability to continue fight-

section. In Chapter Five, we will present both original empirical analysis and existing literature examining the consequences of sanctions on Iran.

TABLE 2.2

Vignettes Demonstrating Effects of Shocks on Military Capability

Vignette	Effects of Shock on Military Capability	Kinetic Interdiction
Confederate industrial and financial constraints (U.S. Civil War)	Severely constrained capability generation; imposed costs	Yes
U.S. rubber supply (WWII)	Severely constrained capability generation; diverted efforts to shock management; imposed costs	Yes
German oil supply (WWII)	Severely constrained capability generation; diverted efforts to shock management; imposed costs	Yes
British Shipbuilding (circa 1980s)	Increased risk to capability generation; imposed costs	No
Cornered markets—i.e., critical materials (circa 2010)	Increased risk to capability generation; diverted efforts to shock management; imposed costs	No
U.S. Budget Control Act (2013)	Increased risk to capability generation	No
U.S. access to Russian RD-180 engines (circa 2014)	Increased risk to capability generation; diverted efforts to shock management; imposed costs; increased trade-offs between national imperatives	No
Effects of energy price drop on Russia (2014–2016)	Delayed capability generation	No
COVID-19 DIB disruptions—e.g., Australian shipbuilding (2020)	Delayed capability generation	No
Hypothetical mobilization	Severely constrains capability generation	No

ing. Insufficient access to oil forced Germany to curtail air and motorized operations.

The vignettes on the effects of the energy price drop on Russia (2014–2016) and COVID-19 DIB disruptions—e.g., Australian shipbuilding (2020), demonstrate the potential of economic shocks to delay the fielding of military capability. Russia delayed defense modernization programs in response to the fiscal pressures caused by reduced energy prices. Defense programs such as Australia's shipbuilding efforts were delayed by disruptions stemming from the COVID-19 pandemic. The military consequences of these delays are circumstance dependent and challenging to quantify, in part because the delays did not occur simultaneously with mobilization or combat. If they had, such delays could have resulted in severe and potentially decisive military disadvantage. The hypothetical mobilization vignette directly investigates this possibility. But even during peacetime, such delays could cause concrete—if hard-to-measure—military damage. For instance, delayed modernization or fielding could meaningfully detract from deterrence, potentially leading to more-aggressive posturing by adversaries or forcing the diversion of resources to fill the deterrence gap.

The three vignettes on British shipbuilding (circa 1980s), cornered markets—i.e., critical materials (circa 2010), and U.S. access to Russian RD-180 engines (circa 2014) illustrate situations in which national defense depended upon sources of supply that were geographically concentrated and nondomestic. In all three situations, this dependence increased the risk of denied access to war materiel. It is difficult to quantify the actual military damage that resulted in these situations because the shocks did not occur simultaneously with mobilization or conflict, but the potential for damage is clear. The United States might have lost access to critical space launch capability had it not made an exception to sanctions policy and allowed RD-180 purchases from Russia. As with the above vignettes on program delays, had the diminishment of British shipbuilding capability or Japanese access to critical materials occurred during mobilization or military conflict, the damage could have been severe. Even during peacetime, the potential of denied access could have changed the strategic or tactical behavior of these countries or their geopolitical adversaries.

Evidence of Resource Diversion and Increased Trade-Offs with Other Imperatives

In several of the vignettes, an important consequence of the underlying shock was the diversion of resources to manage their effects. All three of the vignettes involving kinetic action—Confederate industrial and financial constraints (U.S. Civil War), the U.S. rubber supply (WWII), and the German oil supply (WWII)—feature indirect shock effects as affected combatants diverted resources from other war efforts to alleviate supply restrictions. Civilian populations also faced limited access to, or increasing costs for, dual-use goods and inputs. We do not have evidence to evaluate whether increased costs to civilian populations had measurable consequences in these situations, but one could imagine that severe privation of civilians caused by prioritization of military requirements could undermine civilian support for war efforts.

In the cases of British Shipbuilding (circa 1980s), cornered markets—i.e., critical materials (circa 2010), the U.S. Budget Control Act (2013), and COVID-19 DIB disruptions—e.g., Australian Shipbuilding (2020), shock management required the investment of financial resources and thus increased trade-offs between defense capability and other public imperatives. For instance, the investments had to be funded through means such as reducing other types of public spending, increasing taxes, or increasing borrowing. Again, we lack direct evidence of the military consequences of these situations, but, in general, fiscal constraints could translate into damagingly tight military budgets or could undermine civilian support for military spending.

The case of U.S. access to Russian RD-180 engines (circa 2014) is especially interesting because, in this vignette, achieving U.S. national security interests through imposing sanctions was at odds with maintaining defense capability. The trade-off here did not fall between civilian and military objectives but rather between the aims of two differing national security priorities.

Conclusion: Economic Shocks Have the Potential to Cause Meaningful Damage to Defense Postures, Similar to the Damage Caused by Kinetic Interdiction

As summarized in our high-level findings across the ten vignettes listed in Table 2.2, economic shocks have the potential to meaningfully compromise military objectives in much the same way as classical kinetic supply interdiction. Across the vignettes, we found instances in which shocks restricted supply, diverted resources, and increased trade-offs with other imperatives—all of which are the objectives of kinetic supply interdiction efforts.

Finding 2: A Modest Portfolio of Analytic Capabilities Would Support Many Objectives That Defense Decisionmakers Might Have for Efforts to Manage the Consequences of Economic Shocks

To determine how defense decisionmakers could benefit from a capability to analyze economic shocks, we consider three questions for each vignette. First, what objectives might defense decisionmakers have in managing the consequences of economic shocks? We categorize these objectives into three groups, which we call *management foci*. Second, what data-derived insights might decisionmakers find valuable in designing, selecting, and implementing courses of action to achieve their objectives? We call distinct types of insight *analytic capability requirements*. Third, what distinct analyses are required to achieve each analytic capability requirement? We phrase each analysis in the form of the question that each distinct analysis must answer and call these *analytic questions*. The distinction between analytic capability requirements and analytic questions might seem subtle. Analytic capability requirements specify the outputs of an analytic process—that is, what decisionmakers might want to know. Analysis questions specify a hypothesis or research question that analytic methods must help answer. Meanwhile, the management foci associate decisionmaker objectives with relevant subsets of analytic capability requirements. Figure 2.1 summarizes the relationship between these three constructs.

Management Foci

The vignettes illustrate a wide range of threats, challenges, and opportunities that economic shocks pose to U.S. defense postures. We categorize these shock consequences into the following three groups that we call *management foci*, because they describe central concerns of potential defense management efforts:

- **Supply restriction:** Shock renders war materiel unavailable or more costly.
- **Inference of government priorities:** For shocks inducing changes in government budget constraints, observing reallocation choices can reveal government priorities and the dynamics underlying those priorities.

FIGURE 2.1

Three Steps to Deriving from the Vignettes a Preliminary Set of Goals for a Department of Defense Capability to Analyze Economic Shocks

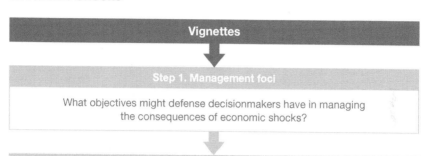

Vignettes

Step 1. Management foci

What objectives might defense decisionmakers have in managing the consequences of economic shocks?

Step 2. Analytic capability requirements

What data-derived insights might decisionmakers find valuable in designing, selecting, and implementing COAs to achieve their objectives?

Step 3. Analysis questions

What distinct analyses are required to achieve each analytic capability requirement?

- **Extreme responses to shocks:** Response within a shocked country is uncommonly severe—e.g., civil unrest, regime change, or military aggression.

Table 2.3 shows the management foci illustrated by each of the 12 vignettes. We turn next to describing each management focus through discussion of the associated vignettes.

Supply Restriction

The central challenge of most of the vignettes we studied is *supply restriction*: the temporary or persistent unavailability of war materiel or the increased cost of obtaining the war materiel (whether cost is measured in terms of price or in terms of trade-offs with other imperatives). Our analysis of the vignettes suggests that economic shocks—or, in some cases, a series of economic shocks—can restrict the supply of war materiel in several ways.

TABLE 2.3

Vignettes Suggest Three Management Foci of Economic Shocks

Vignettes	Supply Restriction	Inference of Government Priorities	Extreme Responses
Confederate industrial and financial constraints (U.S. Civil War)	X		
U.S. rubber supply (WWII)	X		
German oil supply (WWII)	X		
British Shipbuilding (circa 1980s)	X		
Iraqi invasion of Kuwait (1990)			X
Cornered markets—i.e., critical materials (circa 2010)	X		
U.S. sanctions on Iran (2011–2020)	X	X	X
U.S. Budget Control Act (2013)	X	X	
U.S. access to Russian RD-180 engines (circa 2014)	X		
Effects of energy price drop on Russia (2014–2016)	X	X	
COVID-19 DIB disruptions—e.g., Australian shipbuilding (2020)	X		
Hypothetical mobilization scenario	X		

Economic shocks have the potential to inhibit access to war materiel needed immediately to conduct military operations. This is the direct source of military damage in three of the vignettes: Confederate industrial and financial constraints (U.S. Civil War), the German oil supply (WWII), and hypothetical mobilization. In each of these vignettes, resource constraints stemming from a shock limit military commanders' combat options.

Economic shocks also have the potential to delay access to military capability that is not needed immediately but might be needed in the future. Delayed access creates risk of a capability gap in the event of unexpected mobilization. Not only does that potential capability gap create risk of future damage, but it also can undermine deterrence in the present. This was the central concern in the vignettes on COVID-19 DIB disruptions—e.g., Australian shipbuilding (2020) and the effects of the energy price drop on Russia (2014–2016). These shocks delayed modernization programs, potentially leaving readiness and deterrence gaps.

In at least three vignettes, critical damage from the shock was due to increased trade-offs of materiel supply. In the vignette on the U.S. rubber supply (WWII), to maintain military rubber supply, the United States spent tremendous time and resources developing synthetic rubber, in addition to rationing U.S. civilian rubber use. In the vignette on U.S. access to Russian RD-180 engines (circa 2014), the United States had to compromise its objective to exert economic pressure on Russia to maintain a critical space capability. The vignette on U.S. sanctions on Iran (2011–2020) offers another example. One intent of U.S. sanctions was to delay Iranian access to nuclear weapons capability by imposing economic, social, and political costs on pursuing capability in the hope that Iran would decide that the cost of developing nuclear capability was not worth the benefits.

In most of the vignettes featuring supply restriction, a fundamental problem was that the lack of diversified production rendered a critical share of the country's military supply vulnerable to disruption.[9] Several vignettes demonstrate that the risk posed by geographically concentrated supply can be a condition that emerges over time and creates the risk of future damage. Immediate supply restriction was not the central concern of the shocks underlying the vignettes on British Shipbuilding (circa 1980s), cornered markets—i.e., critical materials (circa 2010), and the U.S. Budget Control Act (2013) but rather the risk that increased geographical concentration could increase the risk of future supply restriction.

Inference of Government Priorities

Government spending must be financed through a combination of tax revenue and borrowing. The status of a government's spending, tax revenue, and borrowing positions is called its *fiscal position*. A variety of economic

---

[9] It happens to be case that most of the vignettes feature situations in which production was not just undiversified but was also geographically concentrated in foreign countries and therefore was vulnerable to policy decisions that disrupted trade. But domestic geographical concentration could also create risk of supply restriction—for instance, if natural disaster disrupted production.

shocks can disrupt one element of the government's fiscal position, forcing changes to the other elements. For instance, if a shock decreases tax revenue, then either spending must decrease or borrowing must increase. How the government balances its budget is typically a matter of policy choice subject to external constraints: Through some political decisionmaking process, the government can choose whether, by how much, and where to cut spending or increase borrowing if tax revenues suffer a shock. This decision will reflect government priorities. For instance, perhaps a government chooses to protect certain groups in the population from tax increases or reductions in public services or protects certain defense programs from budget cuts. These choices might reveal government priorities that might not otherwise have been apparent to outside observers.

Three vignettes motivate this management focus. In the vignette on the effects of the energy price drop on Russia (2014–2016), oil price reductions greatly reduced the Russian government's revenue, forcing the Russian government to change its fiscal policy. Likewise, in the vignette on U.S. sanctions on Iran (2011–2020), the sanctions reduced the Iranian government's oil revenue, increased the prices of many imported goods and services, and degraded overall economic conditions, all of which contributed to significant fiscal strain on the Iranian government. In the vignette on the U.S. Budget Control Act (2013), the U.S. government was forced to quickly cut spending because Congress could not agree on a package of tax increases and targeted budget cuts. In all three of these situations, the government's choices of how to manage shocks affecting one element of its fiscal position forced it to make decisions about how to change those other elements, potentially revealing information about the priorities, constraints, and limitations that those governments were facing.

Extreme Responses

The final management focus is the risk that a country suffering an economic shock responds in a way that is very rare and has very high costs—what we call an *extreme response*. An economic shock could degrade the country's well-being so severely, and the effects of the shock could be so challenging to mitigate, that the population or government might undertake high-risk and high-cost responses. Whether or not the United States suffers such economic shocks, extreme responses in other countries have the potential to compromise U.S. security interests.

This focus might most easily be understood in comparison to the prior focus of inferring government priorities from economic shocks that force fiscal policy changes. Both categories involve economic shocks inducing fiscal pressure, perhaps through the deterioration of aggregate economic conditions, which subsequently stress government budgets. The fiscal policy changes envisioned in the previous category—reducing spending or increasing taxes or borrowing—can be described as linear changes, since the degree of fiscal policy change will scale in proportion to the severity of the fiscal pressure. The government can make fiscal policy changes proportionate to the size of the fiscal challenge and is unlikely to increase taxes or cut spending by substantially more than is needed to compensate for tax revenue loss from an economic shock.

In contrast, this final category incorporates responses that are nonlinear, in that there might be no observable changes in, say, the level of civil discord or military aggression until some threshold level of shock severity is passed, beyond which massive changes suddenly occur.

Three vignettes motivate our inclusion of this focus. One vignette, on the Iraqi invasion of Kuwait (1990), provides a historical example of an extreme response: Iraq responded to its economic challenges with military aggression, invading its neighbor Kuwait in an attempt to coerce Kuwait and other Organization of the Petroleum Exporting Countries (OPEC) member nations into alleviating Iraq's economic condition.

For the other two vignettes, economic shocks created conditions that one could imagine might trigger extreme responses. In the vignette on the effects of the energy price drop on Russia (2014–2016), Russia was able to draw from its National Reserve Fund to partially compensate for this budget deficit. But if it did not find other sources of revenue, it might have faced steep budget cuts if energy prices dropped again before it could rebuild its National Reserve Fund. The prospect of steep budget cuts might present such severe consequences that Russia or its population might have undertaken extreme and risky actions. For instance, a substantial share of Russia's population relies on pensions and other transfers and subsidies from the central government for basic living necessities. One could imagine a situation in which budget pressure from future economic shocks presented the

Russian government with the stark choice of cutting the funding for basic necessities upon which much of the population relies. Alternatively, the government might opt to cut other important government goods or services, such as military capability, or to seek revenue from sources that it had previously deemed undesirable. Similarly, in the vignette on U.S. sanctions on Iran (2011–2020), one could imagine that sanctions could create such dire economic conditions in Iran that either the government or the population might undertake extreme actions.

Analytic Capability Requirements and Analysis Questions for Each Management Focus

Having grouped decisionmaker objectives into three management foci, we next turn to identifying the data-derived insights, or analytic capability requirements, that decisionmakers might find valuable for each. Tables 2.4 through 2.7 list analytic capability requirements and associated analysis questions for the management foci. In keeping with the exploratory nature of this project, we offer these as preliminary, not conclusive, lists of analytic capability requirements and analysis questions. In some cases, we judge analytic capability requirements too complex to propose analytic questions without first undertaking additional research that is beyond the scope of this project.

A Note on the Use of the Word "Prediction" in Describing Analytic Capability Requirements

Throughout the remainder of this report, in describing several of the proposed capability requirements, we use the word *prediction* and related words, such as *forecast*. The use of these words deserves some explanation because these words have several subtly distinct meanings. In particular, different disciplines use words such as *prediction* to describe subtly different objectives, and common usage of such words is similarly ambiguous.

In some technical applications and in common usage, a prediction often signifies a single guess about future conditions upon which a decision will be based: What will the weather be at a specific time in the future? Which team will win a game? Relatedly, in many data science applications, prediction refers to classification based on incomplete information: leveraging available data to assign an individual instance of something to one of several mutually exclusive categories. But in the mathematics underlying regression analysis—a commonly used tool in data analysis, economics, statistics, and physical sciences—the word *prediction* often refers to an observed relationship between variables.

One criticism of efforts to make predictions in complex systems is that empirical analysis can be poorly suited to evaluating *black swan* events—events that are uncommon and improbable.[10] A criticism of *prediction* is that because analysis is based on historical data, it might fail to include instances of black swan events precisely because they occur so infrequently. This critique is particularly important in the case of economic shocks: Market participants might change their behavior and adapt to the occurrence of a shock, so that the same shock occurring a second time might not have the same effects (and, in fact, subsequent occurrences might not even be shocking).

In this report, *prediction* and related words, such as *forecast*, refer to the task of making guesses about future conditions by exploiting available data. There are two distinguishing features of the outcomes of predictive tasks envisioned in this report. First, quantification of the uncertainty of predictions is a central output of the prediction efforts envisioned in this report. The objective of predictions in this report is not simply to make a single guess about future outcomes but to estimate the likelihoods of a range of possible outcomes to facilitate the risk management objective underlying this project's efforts.

Second, although a preferred outcome of a larger research effort might be to accurately predict occurrence, timing, and details of specific future events, this initial effort is instead focused on improving decisionmaking through improving decisionmaker understanding of the systems involved in economic shocks. Consequently, the objective of many predictive tasks in this report is not to base decisions on the predictions themselves but to improve understanding of a system by uncovering the relationship between variables. If an empirical model successfully uses one set of variables to predict another, then there is hope that the model contains an accurate representation of the mechanism driving shock occurrence, propagation, or

---

[10] Nassim Nicholas Taleb, *The Black Swan: The Impact of the Highly Improbable*, New York: Random House, 2007.

outcomes. The hope is that this improved understanding can contribute to improved decisionmaking.

Finally, in our view, one benefit of investing in developing the types of frameworks described in Chapter Four is that they incorporate diverse perspectives and approaches, including nonempirical ones, that might address black swan events and—relatedly—nonlinear system relationships that can be hard to empirically study. Even where empirical analysis fails to account for improbable events, it might still be relevant to the vast majority of instances. But, additionally, predictive analysis, as defined in this report, might reveal aspects of mechanisms underlying shock occurrence, propagation, and effects that can be useful for forming expectations about black swan events.

Analytic Capabilities and Questions Relevant to All Three Management Foci

For all management foci, defense decisionmakers may find it helpful to have information enabling them to conduct basic risk management tasks, such as evaluating the risk (probability and severity) of various types of shocks affecting defense postures, detecting shocks as early as possible, and evaluating the effectiveness of any efforts taken to manage the consequences of shocks.

The analytic capability requirements in Table 2.4 address these common needs. To evaluate the probability and the potential severity of damage caused by economic shocks, it will be helpful to be able to identify the shocks to which a DIB, country, economic sector, or trading partner might be directly or indirectly exposed; to be able to estimate the likelihood of shocks occurring or to detect ongoing shocks quickly; to know what system features affect shock outcomes; and to understand the sensitivity of shock outcomes to those system features. It would be particularly useful to understand the sensitivity of shock outcomes to system features that could be the object of management interventions. Finally, it will generally be useful to understand what triggers or instigates shocks, although that form of root-cause analysis can prove very challenging.

TABLE 2.4

Analytic Capability Requirements and Analysis Questions Suggested by Vignettes Relevant to All Management Foci

Analytic Capability Requirement	Analysis Questions
Identifying exposure to and predicting military consequences of a shock	How connected are DIBs to markets exposed to the shock, and with what level of sensitivity?
Detecting shock instances	How can shocks be distinguished from non-shock variation in observable data?
Predicting or detecting ripple effects of shocks on other economic sectors	How connected are other sectors to shocked industries, and with what level of sensitivity?
Predicting or detecting ripple effects of shocks on trading partners	How connected are other countries' economies to shocked industries, and with what level of sensitivity?
Understanding instigation of shock	More foundational analysis is needed.[a]
Identifying factors affecting shock outcomes	What system features drive the nature of shock consequences?
Identifying sensitivity of shock outcomes to those factors	What is the sensitivity of shock outcome severity to system features (or, if market-based, what are relevant price elasticities)?
Identifying points of potential intervention	More foundational analysis is needed.[a]
Estimating the sensitivity of shock outcomes to interventions	What is the sensitivity of shock outcome severity to interventions (or, if market-based, what are relevant price elasticities)?

[a] In the view of the research team, this analytic capability features a particularly high level of complexity or heterogeneity. Consequently, we recommend that more foundational analysis be undertaken to generate a list of associated analytic questions. In many cases, such foundational analysis might take the form of developing frameworks, as discussed in Chapter Three.

Analytic Capabilities and Questions for the Supply Restriction Management Focus

Table 2.5 lists analytic capability requirements and analytic questions that might be especially useful for the supply restriction management focus. This table might be helpful for predicting shock latency, or at least understanding the factors affecting it. The latter is important because it indicates the time available to mitigate shock consequences before suffering damage. Another

TABLE 2.5

Analytic Capability Requirements and Analysis Questions Suggested by Vignettes for the Supply Restriction Management Focus

Analytic Capability Requirement	Analysis Questions
Predicting shock propagation speed	How fast after onset does a shock cause a consequence?
Predicting and detecting supply challenges	What are typical variations in measurable system features and outcomes versus atypical variations indicative of shocks?
Identifying alternative sources of supply or production	Where else are goods and services produced, or where else could they be produced?
Assessing alternative forms of supply or production	More foundational analysis is needed.[a]

[a] In the view of the research team, this analytic capability features a particularly high level of complexity or heterogeneity. Consequently, we recommend that more foundational analysis be undertaken to generate a list of associated analytic questions. In many cases, such foundational analysis might take the form of developing frameworks, as discussed in Chapter Three.

useful capability is detecting and predicting shock consequences themselves, since supply restrictions might be more observable or more informative of management choices than detecting and predicting the shocks themselves. The final two capability requirements in this section target management choices: identifying and accessing alternative sources of supply.

Analytic Capabilities and Questions for the Inference of Government Priorities Management Focus

Analytic capability requirements and analytic questions that are especially helpful for inferring government priorities are listed in Table 2.6. To exploit opportunities to infer government priorities from fiscal policy changes forced by economic shocks, it would be helpful to be able to characterize changes in taxing and spending policy induced by the shock. It is worth noting that some observed changes might not be in response to the shock but merely coinciding with shock timing by coincidence. It would also be helpful to be able to identify constraints that the government faced in changing revenue or spending decisions. For instance, increasing tax rates on market transactions increases market prices, and some consumers will choose not to purchase the good at the higher post-tax price. If too many

TABLE 2.6

Analytic Capability Requirements and Analysis Questions Suggested by Vignettes for the Inference of Government Priorities Management Focus

Analytic Capability Requirement	Analysis Questions
Inferring what observed spending choices indicate about government priorities	Did the government change tax rates anywhere to compensate for revenue lost to shock?
	What limits does the government face in changing tax rates (e.g., high price elasticities of demand in taxable markets)?
	Did the government change budget allocations to preserve some programs?
Connecting inferred priorities to government strategy, intent, or constraints	More foundational analysis is needed.[a]

[a] In the view of the research team, this analytic capability features a particularly high level of complexity or heterogeneity. Consequently, we recommend that more foundational analysis be undertaken to generate a list of associated analytic questions. In many cases, such foundational analysis might take the form of developing frameworks, as discussed in Chapter Three.

consumers choose not to purchase the good, a tax rate increase could actually decrease tax revenue by reducing the number of taxable transactions. Thus, discerning policy choice from policy constraint can require more-sophisticated analysis than might seem to be the case at first blush.

Analytic Capabilities and Questions for the Extreme Responses Management Focus

Finally, Table 2.7 lists the analytic capabilities and associated analysis questions useful for managing the potential of economic shocks to induce extreme responses. We identify two analytic capability requirements. The first is the ability to estimate the risk of a specific extreme response (for instance, regime change or military aggression). This is an extremely difficult question, and we determined that more foundational research is needed just to establish relevant analysis questions. The second analytic capability for this management focus is the ability to anticipate the conditions under which any extreme response might be triggered by an economic shock. Again, this is a complicated undertaking, but we can offer at least a preliminary set of analysis questions. It would be helpful to be able to analyze

TABLE 2.7

Analytic Capability Requirements and Analysis Questions Suggested by Vignettes for the Extreme Response Management Focus

Analytic Capability Requirement	Analysis Questions
Estimating the risk of a particular extreme response to some shock	More foundational analysis is needed.[a]
Evaluating the risk that a particular shock will lead to some extreme response	How will shock affect key macroeconomic indicators, key economic sectors, and key political constituencies?
	Could decisionmakers perceive the potential benefits of an extreme response as outweighing the costs of such extreme responses?
	How sensitive is the country's stability to shocks in selected industries (i.e., dependence on a key industrial input, government spending program, trade partner, foreign reserves, tax revenue source, etc.)?

[a] In the view of the research team, this analytic capability features a particularly high level of complexity or heterogeneity. Consequently, we recommend that more foundational analysis be undertaken to generate a list of associated analytic questions. In many cases, such foundational analysis might take the form of developing frameworks, as discussed in Chapter Three.

a country's economic and fiscal profile to evaluate how close the population is to subsistence-level consumption and how sensitive household income is to changes in policy-sensitive consumption bundles, such as energy or food subsidies. This might indicate situations in which there are high and especially contentious trade-offs between civil and military spending. For example, is there sufficient budgetary headroom to provide necessities, such as food, to the population while maintaining military spending?

Conclusion: A Modest Portfolio of Analytic Capabilities Would Support Many Objectives That Defense Decisionmakers Might Have for Efforts to Manage the Consequences of Economic Shocks

Given the numerous ways economic shocks might affect defense postures, and the correspondingly numerous potential objectives of management efforts, it is not a foregone conclusion that there is a path to providing cost-effective analytic support to defense decisionmakers. However, we propose that despite the expansiveness of the challenge, there are common mechanisms underlying the occurrence, propagation, and effects of shocks, which, in turn, relate to decisionmaker objectives. In particular, we propose three management foci that account for many of the objectives that defense decisionmakers will have in managing the consequences of economic shocks. Then, we propose a finite list of analytic capability requirements that would contribute meaningfully to those management foci and propose a finite list of analysis questions that would help achieve the analytic capability requirements. While the management foci, analytic capability requirements, and analysis questions we propose will not comprehensively address all of the analytic needs of defense decisionmakers, we argue that they would provide a substantial amount of useful information.

CHAPTER THREE

How Well Do Existing Methods Achieve the Required Analytic Capabilities?

In Chapter Two, we proposed analytic capability requirements for data-informed management of the consequences of economic shocks. In this chapter, we assess the extent to which existing analytic methods meet those requirements. First, we discuss the technical challenges to achieving the required capabilities. Second, we discuss how economics research approaches shocks and detail four workhorse empirical methods developed in that body of literature. In the final section of this chapter, we conduct a gap analysis in which we examine the extent to which existing empirical methods overcome the technical challenges and satisfy the analytic capability requirements.

Technical Challenges to Achieving the Analytic Capability Requirements

Most of the analytic capability requirements presented in Chapter Two are variations of this question: How can we leverage one observable feature to predict[1] another? In many cases, this question has an additional causal element that adds to the challenge: How does one system feature not just predict but also affect another one? Answering these questions with high

---

[1] See Chapter Two for a discussion of the meaning of *prediction* in this report.

precision, accuracy, and confidence, and, therefore, obtaining high-quality empirical outputs, requires overcoming four technical challenges:

1. identifying the mathematical structure of the relationship between the system features
2. determining whether empirical results provide meaningful information about the relationship between system features, as opposed to capturing correlations appearing by random chance
3. accounting for changes in relationship between the two system features that might occur over time, especially as components of the system adapt to shocks and other changing conditions
4. assessing whether the relationship is measured with sufficient accuracy to support decisionmaking.

Identifying the Mathematical Structure of the Relationship Between the System Features

In terms of the first challenge, identifying the mathematical structure of relationships between system variables can be challenging because there is such a wide range of potential relationships, and available data might not help distinguish between those potential relationships. In the simplest case, two variables have a linear relationship with each other: A change in variable X is always associated with a proportional change in variable Y. But relationships can be far more complicated. For example, perhaps the relationship is exponential, so that for small values of X, small changes in X are associated with small changes in Y, but for large values of X, small changes in X are associated with very large changes in Y. Or perhaps there is a positive correlation between X and Y for some values of X, but a negative correlation for other values of X. Or perhaps there is no correlation between X and Y except above a certain threshold value of X. The number of potential mathematical relationships is infinite.

In many applied science and engineering applications, the nature of important mathematical relationships between system features has been established through controlled experiments. Mathematical relationships for many of the economic, political, and other behavioral phenomena envisioned in this study are not well known. In a very simple system, the mathematical structure of the relationship between two variables would be easy to establish by simply looking at how the two variables vary with each other using data visualization or any of a number of curve-fitting mathematical techniques. However, economic shocks generally occur in complex systems, giving rise to the second challenge that complicates this investigation.

Determining Whether Empirical Results Provide Meaningful Information About the Relationship Between System Features

The second challenge is that, in highly complex systems, such as economies, business processes, production processes, and supply chains, there are tremendous numbers of system features—some of which are unobservable, and some of which are stochastic, or subject to random variation—that will influence the features that are the subject of an analysis. As a result, system features will almost always have some random variation (*noise*) in them so that the exact correlation between X and Y will vary somewhat from one observation to another. Consequently, even if variables X and Y are closely related to each other, they will have at least slightly inconsistent correlations with each other because no two situations in which one measures variables X and Y will be exactly the same with respect to all observed and unobserved system features.

If the basic nature of the relationship between two variables were known—if it was known that X and Y had a linear relationship or that Y was an exponential value of X, for instance—then, given enough observations, widely used statistical methods could be used to infer the exact relationship between X and Y despite the random variation. Statistical methods are empirical methods that strive to characterize system features that are subject to random variation by extrapolating from a subset of observable data. Put differently, statistical methods seek to quantify the extent to which characteristics of observable data can be used to characterize similar data that are not observable or have not yet occurred. Even under ideal conditions, such inference would still be subject to uncertainty, since there would still be a chance—however unlikely—that the statistical methods were inaccurately identifying random chance outcomes as a significant relationship between variables. But if the underlying mathematical model is correctly selected, at least this risk of false attribution could be quantified for decisionmakers.[2]

Accounting for Changes in Relationship Between the Two System Features That Might Occur Over Time, Especially as Components of the System Adapt to Shocks and Other Changing Conditions

The third challenge is that even when a relationship between system variables is successfully discovered, even with a high degree of confidence, it is subject to change. In the specific case of economic shocks, decisionmakers in a shocked economy or market may adapt to an economic shock in a way that changes their behavior in the event of a future shock, or an earlier shock might deplete resources available to weather a later shock, so that future shocks do not have the same consequences as past shocks.

Similarly, decisionmakers might alter resource allocations in response to other types of system-wide events, which incidentally alter the effects of subsequent shocks. An important example in the context of this study is a comparison of how shocks might affect a DIB in peacetime versus wartime. The DIB for a given defense capability might differ during peacetime and wartime in many ways that have implications for how economic shocks affect defense postures. To take one such example, when large-scale combat operations increase defense requirements, some firms that produced only civilian goods during peacetime will transition production to military goods. There might have been differences in exposure and resilience to economic shocks between the types of firms that were in the DIB during peacetime and those that were not. For instance, perhaps firms that were in the DIB during peacetime tended to be older, larger, and more financially stable than firms with similar production capabilities that were not in the DIB. Economic mobilization would therefore change the composition of firms in the DIB, increasing the share of production at risk from the types of economic shocks that are more likely to disrupt the production of these newcomers.

---

[2] A common way to express the level of uncertainty over an estimate is in the form of a confidence interval.

Summarizing the discussion of technical challenges so far, the first three challenges amplify each other: If systems features were fully observable and nonstochastic (that is, not subject to random variation), then mathematical relationships between features would be straightforward to establish. If the mathematical relationships between features were known and there were sufficient data, then the exact relationship between the parameters could be estimated with a known level of confidence. Because system relationships are subject to change, it is difficult to distinguish between random variation and a changing relationship, complicating inference and undermining the external validity of analytic outputs. Many of the scenarios under consideration in the analysis of economic shocks will suffer from all three challenges.

Assessing Whether the Relationship Is Measured with Sufficient Accuracy to Support Decisionmaking

The fourth fundamental technical challenge is that often it will be infeasible to base analysis solely on the situation of interest to decisionmakers. The risk is that analytical output derived from training on other data or similar but not exact prior conditions will not necessarily be valid when applied to the scenario of interest. For instance, insights based on analysis using data from one country (e.g., an industrialized democracy) might not apply to other countries with different economic structures or governance institutions (e.g., an agrarian autocracy) because mechanisms of shock propagation might vary depending on economic structure. Similarly, analysis based on historical data might not be valid in future situations if underlying economic features have changed. Unfortunately, given the complexity of the systems involved in the propagation of economic shocks to outcomes of interest—the multiplicity of factors and the challenges of measuring them—it can be hard to assess the external validity of analytic outputs and therefore quantify the confidence that decisionmakers should put in them, especially when using purely data-driven analysis.

How the Technical Obstacles Manifest During Analysis

Practically speaking, these challenges often manifest as decisions that need to be made about how to structure analyses for a given situation. Some key empirical details requiring appropriate specification in the face of the above technical challenges include the following:

- **How should shocks be defined and measured?** Shocks change market participants' evaluation of factors underlying a business decision, so the definition of shock should capture what participants view as new information. In some cases, any change in the level of measured activity reflects the magnitude of shock, but, in other cases, the relationship might be more complicated. For instance, for a system feature that usually has high variation, perhaps only extreme changes qualify as shocks. Defining shocks as any change in activity might require a different mathematical representation than defining shocks as only extreme changes in the level.

- **On which measurable outcomes of shocks should an analysis focus?** Outcomes of interest to defense decisionmakers will vary across contexts. For some markets, defense decisionmakers might be concerned with how a shock affects the number of firms in the industry. In another instance, decisionmakers might be concerned with product price. Outcomes of interest must reflect whatever risk defense decisionmakers are managing, and there are many different outcomes that might be useful across the full range of analyses and situations.

- **What system features or events have the potential to affect shock outcomes? What is the level of sensitivity of shock outcomes to these features?** There are at least two aspects of this set of questions. First, the effects of shocks on the outcome variables of interest might vary across different measurable system features. Shocks might affect small businesses and large businesses differently, and a model that does not account for this difference will be inaccurate. Second, incorporating system features can sometimes reduce the uncertainty associated with parameter estimates in statistical inference. A useful empirical model replicates the essential dynamics driving how shocks cause important changes in the outcome of interest. Shock measurement, outcome selection, feature selection, and—especially—empirical model selection all reflect aspects of these dynamics. As discussed above, the model must capture the mathematical relationship between the shock and outcome variable sufficiently well to give accurate results. If time matters to the effect of shocks, then the model must also embed a time dimension. For instance, as discussed in the next section, time considerations might drive the choice between an I-O model or a computable general equilibrium (CGE) model. A model might also capture time by defining the outcome variable as change measured over a key period of time, or a model might include time as an explanatory variable.

- **Can empirical analysis achieve the required level of precision across a range of data environments?** Each of the above modeling choices can be implemented only if appropriate data are available. Lack of available data might preclude certain modeling features. For instance, if the ideal model of shock propagation would incorporate daily data, but data are only available monthly, a model might lose accuracy, precision, or even relevance. Poor data quality, with missing or inaccurate observations, can affect model accuracy (causing the model to give misleading results) or can reduce model precision (leading to less confidence in results).

- **Is the analysis robust to adaptations and other structural changes that might occur between shock instances?** Changes in measured relationships over time will reduce the validity of predictions based on past instances. Analysis might need to identify the risk of adaptation driving prediction error. However, all is not lost because adaptations might themselves be predictable based either on analogous situations or on a sufficiently detailed understanding of system dynamics.

In short, a precursor to creating analytic capability is establishing consistent approaches to defining, identifying, measuring, and modeling economic shocks and their effects. To the best of our knowledge, there has not been a comprehensive, systematic investigation into the empirical modeling of the effects of economic shocks on defense postures. Consequently, we look to the economics literature on shocks to evaluate the extent to which these approaches have been established through prior research.

Existing Methodological Capabilities

Many disciplines draw on empirical analyses inferring relationships between system features. The economics literature has a large corpus of research specifically on shocks and has grappled with many of the technical challenges discussed above. We examined this subset of the economics literature, focusing most closely on the empirical methods used across different types of shocks. Appendix A details our review of the economics literature, which included a survey of how the economics literature defines and statistically identifies shocks and an in-depth, comprehensive review of the literature of four specific types of shocks: oil, agriculture and trade, finance, and labor. Our objective in this literature review was to characterize the capabilities of currently available ("existing") empirical methods in order to ascertain whether advancements in empirical methodologies are needed to satisfy the analytic capability requirements identified in Chapter Two.

Our main finding from this literature review is that four types of existing empirical methods (which we refer to in this report as *workhorse methods* because of their frequent usage in the economics literature on shocks) are used widely across all of the types of shocks we examined. While many different empirical methods are used across the economics literature, these four methods are used with striking frequency across many different types of shocks and to approach many different research questions. These methods are VAR models, I-O models, CGE models, and panel regression (PR) models—a category that for the purposes of this report includes reduced-form causal inference models.[3] Each of these methods examines shocks from a different angle. Figure 3.1 presents summary explanations of the four models and provides a notional example of applications of each. These examples draw on the vignette on U.S. sanctions against Iran, an example that we will cover in greater depth in Chapter Four. Appendix B provides

---

[3] Not all PR models are used for reduced-form causal inference. Furthermore, reduced-form causal inference does not necessarily entail the use of PR models. However, many of the papers we reviewed used PR models to achieve reduced-form causal analysis, so we grouped these together without further explanation to avoid unnecessary complexity in this report.

FIGURE 3.1

Summary of the Four Workhorse Empirical Methods Used to Study Shocks in Economics

Example applications from
Iran sanctions use case

How do sanctions affect Iran's macroeconomy and government spending over five years?	**Vector autoregression (VAR)** • Stochastic process model; captures interdependencies among a set of time series • Useful for assessing how the effects of shocks are likely to evolve over time • Requires time series data of shock and outcomes of interest
How do sanctions immediately affect sectors of Iran's economy and Iran's trading partners?	**Input-output (I-O) models** • Quantify the connectedness among sectors/firms in national/regional/world economy • Useful for examining immediate spillovers but cannot capture adaptations to shocks • Data availability varies by country and supply chain
How do sanctions affect Iran's industrial landscape several years later, after the economy has adjusted?	**Computable general equilibrium (CGE) models** • Economy-wide, simulation-based optimization models • Useful for examining longer-run spillovers by simulating adaptations to shocks • Extremely data and computationally intensive; can be very situation specific
How do sanction-induced reductions in food support affect infant and maternal health outcomes?	**Panel regression models/reduced-form causal inference** • Broad class of models applied to data on units that are tracked over time • Flexible class of models; calculates the causal effects of one variable on another, such as the effect of a shock on a specific outcome of interest • Can be applied only under very limited, context-dependent circumstances

detail on each of the four methods beyond what is discussed in the sections below.

As suggested by Figure 3.1, these methods are not necessarily in competition with each other. Instead, each offers a different type of insight into the consequences of a shock. Our literature review identified the most widely used methods for achieving various useful insights. Consequently, these methods sit at the intersection of methods that have been well validated and are widely accepted and those that are the most modern or state of the art for achieving their particular aims.[4]

Vector Autoregression

VAR models offer the advantage of being able to both measure shocks and forecast their effects. Moreover, their dynamic nature allows one to assess how the effects of shocks are likely to evolve over successive days, weeks, months, quarters, or years, depending on the frequency of the data feeding the model. This allows the researcher to ascertain the projected time between shock onset and its effects, as well as the duration and magnitude of shock effects. VARs have been employed widely, and we list just a few instances here. Kilian, 2009, used a structural vector autoregression (SVAR) to identify oil supply and demand shocks and forecast their effect on oil prices.[5] Bakas and Triantafyllou, 2018, employed this approach to study how uncertainty affects commodities price volatility.[6] Vuolteenaho, 2002, constructed a VAR to project the effect of cash-flow and expected-return news on firm stock returns.[7] Canova, Coutinho, and Kontolemis, 2012, examined the role played by institutional factors and product market reforms in explaining how sectors in the European Union respond to economic shocks.[8] They also exploit the frame-

---

[4] As the literature review in Appendix B illustrates, in some cases, the most modern, widely accepted methods are several decades old (e.g., VAR). Also, it is important to know that these workhorse methods have many different variations. For example, Bayesian structural vector autoregressions (BSVARs) are a variation of VARs. These variations are sometimes incremental improvements on the original method, but, more often, the variations are tailored to perform optimally in a very specific context. Regardless, we consider the original, widely used, and widely accepted method to be the workhorse method for clarity of exposition.

[5] Lutz Kilian, "Not All Oil Price Shocks Are Alike: Disentangling Demand and Supply Shocks in the Crude Oil Market," *American Economic Review*, Vol. 99, No. 3, 2009.

[6] Dimitrios Bakas and Athanasios Triantafyllou, "The Impact of Uncertainty Shocks on the Volatility of Commodity Prices," *Journal of International Money and Finance*, Vol. 87, 2018.

[7] Tuomo Vuolteenaho, "What Drives Firm-Level Stock Returns?" *Journal of Finance*, Vol. 57, No. 1, 2002.

[8] Fabio Canova, Leonor Coutinho, and Zenon G. Kontolemis, *Measuring the Macroeconomic Resilience of Industrial Sectors in the EU and Assessing the Role of Product*

work to quantify sector- and country-level resilience to shocks. This selection of papers demonstrates the breadth of questions to which VARs are able to speak. However, VARs are relatively less well suited to explicitly capturing and tracing out *spillover effects*—how a shock to one firm or sector spreads through other firms or sectors.

Input-Output

I-O models are well suited to answering questions about spillover effects of shocks, especially immediately after the shock and before entities have had a chance to adjust to post-shock conditions, because they quantify the level of connectedness between sectors or firms in a national or regional economy. More specifically, they capture the degree to which the goods and services produced by each sector or firm serve as inputs to the production processes of other sectors or firms. A core feature of I-O models is their ability to trace how a change in the output of a given entity affects other entities through backward supply chain linkages, ultimately allowing researchers to project the aggregate influence of a relatively isolated initial disruption. I-O models have traditionally been used to estimate the effects of sector-level shocks, as analysis at this level is directly supported by public data collection efforts. However, more-recent work has applied the overarching concept to model firm-level networks. For example, Albino, Izzo, and Kühtz, 2002, developed an approach to examine production flows in global supply chains and between local segments of broader supply chains.[9] Carvalho et al., 2016, built on the I-O linkages concept to estimate the role that supplier-customer relationships played in amplifying and propagating the economic shock caused by the Great East Japan Earthquake of 2011.[10] Firm-level I-O models have the capability to inform multiple dimensions of supply chain

Market Regulations, Vol. 112, Luxembourg: Publications Office of the European Union, 2012.

[9]   Vito Albino, Carmen Izzo, and Silvana Kühtz, "Input–Output Models for the Analysis of a Local/Global Supply Chain," *International Journal of Production Economics*, Vol. 78, No. 2, 2002.

[10]   Vasco M. Carvalho, Makoto Nirei, Yukiko U. Saito, and Alireza Tahbaz-Salehi, "DP11711 Supply Chain Disruptions: Evidence from the Great East Japan Earthquake," working paper, 2016.

risk management (SCRM). These models can shed light on questions such as (1) the centrality of a given firm in a supply chain, (2) how a given disruption would be expected to ripple through the supply chain, (3) which types of disruptions would be expected to have the greatest effect on a supply chain, and (4) how vulnerable a supply chain is to disruptions at the geographic level. Point 4 might be especially useful for examining the spillover effects of geographically concentrated shocks because an I-O model would allow one to estimate how a disruption to all firms in a given geographic area might propagate throughout broader supply chains. I-O models have their drawbacks, which typically include an inability to accurately capture behavioral responses to a disruption (such as input substitution). This can bias their estimates upward when considering long-term disruptions with long-lasting effects. Some of their shortcomings can be addressed by, for example, augmenting the models to explicitly capture resilience.

Computable General Equilibrium

Like I-O models, CGE models also are useful for examining the spillover effects of shocks, but over a longer time period, after entities have had a chance to adjust to post-shock conditions. To accomplish this, in contrast with I-O models, CGE models explicitly account for behavioral adjustments to the shock itself by modeling optimizing behavior. A key implication of this optimization-based structure is that CGE models estimate changes in prices and reactions to those changes. For households, changes in the relative prices of goods and services affect their income and optimal consumption profiles. For firms, price changes affect their chosen inputs to production—capital, labor, and intermediate goods and services—and, consequently, production levels. CGE models therefore contain rational economic behavior that ultimately serves to mitigate the economic effects of a disruption.[11] Thus, this class of models is relatively better suited to estimating the effects of longer-term disruptions where such behavior is feasible and plausible. CGE models tend to produce similar types of outputs

---

[11] Historically, CGE models have been applied to price-based markets, so equations modeling behavior leans heavily on price. In principle, market prices are not necessary for CGE models as long as the model incorporates some other feature that serves to incentivize market participants and clear markets.

as I-O models, though the latter can be more straightforward to apply at the firm level. Of particular relevance to the topic of this project is the ability of CGE models to estimate resilience. Rose, Oladosu, and Liao, 2007, built a Los Angeles–specific CGE model that estimated sector-level resilience to a total electricity blackout lasting two weeks.[12] In their framework, overall resilience is a function of a number of underlying variables, which can be organized into two categories: inherent resilience and adaptive resilience. The former represents the ability to attenuate the effects of a disruption under normal circumstances, while the latter captures the ability to lessen the effects in crisis scenarios when there is increased impetus to put in extra effort or find creative solutions to blunt the effects of the initial disruption. In principle, this concept could be applied at the firm level to estimate supply chain resilience in a variety of scenarios, such as the COVID-19 pandemic. Pairing CGE-generated resilience estimates with a firm-level I-O model could improve the fidelity of I-O estimates and provide a potentially powerful way to forecast the effects of supply chain disruptions and identify key risk factors.

Panel Regression Models

While there are many different modeling frameworks that fall under the PR umbrella, there are broad commonalities across them in terms of the benefits and drawbacks of their use for SCRM. PR models represent a flexible class of models that can be adapted to a wide range of scenarios. Moreover, their structure allows them to produce relatively precise causal estimates of the effects of an array of economic shocks. Doing so comes at the cost of needing to carefully tailor the model to each scenario of interest. In addition, PR models are generally less well suited to producing dynamic forecasts that allow one to see how effects are expected to evolve over time. They tend to measure the net change in some variable of interest before and after an event occurs without charting the dynamic pathway by which that variable transitions over time between the pre- and post-event values. Chodorow-Reich, 2014, used PR models to study the effect of bank-lending frictions on firm

---

[12] Adam Rose, Gbadebo Oladosu, and Shu-Yi Liao, "Business Interruption Impacts of a Terrorist Attack on the Electric Power System of Los Angeles: Customer Resilience to a Total Blackout," *Risk Analysis: An International Journal*, Vol. 27, No. 3, 2007.

employment outcomes.[13] Costello, 2020, employed PR models to examine how banking sector shocks spread through the corporate economy.[14] Specifically, she documented liquidity spillover effects from constrained suppliers to downstream customers and estimated the consequences for downstream firms. As noted above, PR models are best suited for questions involving specific, precise effects over a fixed time frame.

Gap Analysis

Next, we turn to examining the extent to which the above four workhorse empirical methods used to study shocks in the economics literature satisfy the analytic capability requirements presented in Chapter Two. First, we discuss how the workhorse methods can contribute to answering the analytic questions associated with each capability requirement. Second, we discuss the limitations of those methods, both in terms of which analytic questions the methods do not help address and where the methods only address the questions incompletely or under limited circumstances. Finally, we discuss two methodological advancements that we propose would yield significant improvements in analytic support to defense decisionmakers.

Our analysis leads to three findings:

- **Finding 3:** A small number of workhorse methods from empirical economics can contribute useful analysis to a wide variety of scenarios.
- **Finding 4:** (Gap) The workhorse empirical methods cannot always overcome the technical challenges to achieving the analytic capability requirements.
- **Finding 5:** (Gap) Even if the technical obstacles to achieving the analytic capability requirements in all applied environments were over-

---

[13] Gabriel Chodorow-Reich, "The Employment Effects of Credit Market Disruptions: Firm-Level Evidence from the 2008–9 Financial Crisis," *Quarterly Journal of Economics*, Vol. 129, No. 1, 2014.

[14] Anna M. Costello, "Credit Market Disruptions and Liquidity Spillover Effects in the Supply Chain," *Journal of Political Economy*, Vol. 128, No. 9, 2020.

come, additional analysis would be needed to leverage these empirical insights to inform decisionmaking.

Finding 3: A Small Number of Workhorse Methods from Empirical Economics Can Contribute Useful Analysis to a Wide Variety of Scenarios

The four workhorse empirical methods from economics presented in the previous section—VAR, I-O, CGE, and PR—are useful and perhaps, in some cases, even necessary for answering many of the analytic questions presented in Chapter Two. Table 3.1 lists which of the four workhorse empirical methods can help inform each of the analytic questions presented in Chapter Two. As we discuss in further detail below, the value of each listed method may vary across specific situations, but we propose that, in many situations, the listed models can provide value in answering the associated questions. For instance, looking at the first row of Table 3.1, VARs can potentially identify and measure the magnitude of a causal relationship between a shock and activity in a particular DIB.

Panel models are most challenging to characterize, because this is a broad class of models and the ability to apply a given panel model is very sensitive to data and other contextual features. Consequently, in several places, "panel model" is listed with the quantifier "potentially." Also, one particularly useful form of economic analysis for studying shocks is estimation of elasticities. Elasticity quantifies endogenous relationships between changes in one economic variable and changes in another. A specific example that might help illustrate the value of elasticity is price elasticity of demand or supply: In many cases, a shock will trigger market price changes. Knowing the appropriate elasticity helps to predict the change in market equilibrium that will result from the shock. Panel models are commonly used for estimating price elasticities. The case study presented in Chapter Four provides several concrete examples of the potential applications of several of the methods to address analytic questions.

The broad utility of these four methods leads to our third finding: Out of dozens of available analytic methods, four workhorse methods from economics contribute substantial and important analysis for the management of economic shocks. Our in-depth review of

TABLE 3.1

Workhorse Empirical Methods from Economics Inform Many Analysis Questions

Focus	Analysis Questions	Analysis Method(s)
All	How connected are DIBs to markets exposed to the shock, and with what level of sensitivity?	VAR
	How can shocks be distinguished from non-shock variation in observable data?	VAR, panel models
	How connected are other sectors to shocked industries, and with what level of sensitivity?	I-O, CGE
	How connected are other countries' economies to shocked industries, and with what level of sensitivity?	I-O, CGE
	What system features drive the nature of shock consequences?	Panel models; possibly VAR, I-O, CGE
	What is the sensitivity of shock outcome severity to system features (or, if market-based, to elasticities)?	Panel models
	What is the sensitivity of shock outcome severity to interventions (or, if market based, to elasticities)?	Panel models
Supply restriction	How fast after onset does a shock cause a consequence?	VAR
	What are typical variations in measurable system features and outcomes versus atypical variations indicative of shocks?	Panel models, descriptive statistics
	Where else are goods and services produced, or where else could they be produced?	I-O models
Inference of government priorities	Did the government change tax rates anywhere to compensate for revenue lost to shock?	†
	What limits does the government face in changing tax rates (e.g., high elasticities in taxable markets)?	Panel models to estimate elasticities
	Did the government change budget allocations to preserve some programs?	Possibly panel models

Table 3.1—Continued

Focus	Analysis Questions	Analysis Method(s)
Extreme response	How will shock affect key macroeconomic indicators, key economic sectors, and key political constituencies?	VAR, I-O, CGE; possibly a role for panel models to estimate elasticities
	Can benefits of an extreme response outweigh the costs of such extreme responses?	†
	How sensitive is the country's stability to shocks in selected industries (i.e., dependence on a key industrial input, government spending program, trade partner, foreign reserves, tax revenue source, etc.)?	VAR, I-O, CGE

† Utility of any of the four methods under consideration is unclear. Further foundational analysis is needed.

research on four types of shocks found that the existing research dispro-portionately used these four methods. Likewise, we find these methods broadly applicable across the analytic questions presented in Chapter Two. This finding stands in contrast with the research team's expectation before undertaking the literature analysis: We expected that a much larger set of modeling methods would be needed to achieve such broad coverage of the analytic questions.

Finding 4: (Gap) The Workhorse Empirical Methods Cannot Always Overcome the Technical Challenges to Achieving the Analytic Capability Requirements

While extremely useful and perhaps necessary for answering many of the analytic questions, the workhorse methods are not sufficient. Each method can be used only when certain requirements—particularly those regarding data availability and assumptions about economic dynamics—are met. Also, the methods have limitations in terms of the conclusions that can be drawn from the results they generate.

Requirements and Limitations of VAR

There are several implementation challenges of using VARs. In terms of data, VARs require time series data of variables, each of which is serially correlated with itself and correlated with the other system variables. VARs also require assumptions about relationships between variables that can be challenging to justify.[15] Moreover, VAR result accuracy is sensitive to proper model specification, since the recursive nature of a VAR estimate leads to the compounding of forecast error under model misspecification. A limitation of VARs is that they are relatively less well suited to explicitly capturing and tracing out *spillover effects*—how a shock to one firm or sector spreads through other firms or sectors, since they do not necessarily offer a clear pre-shock baseline measure of the connection between firm, sectors, or countries.

Requirements and Limitations of Input-Output Models

I-O models require data on interlinkages at a suitable level of aggregation to support the analysis. Analysis might require data on linkages between countries, between firms, between industries within a single country or across several countries, etc. Data on linkages at the desired level of analysis might be unavailable. For example, some countries might not offer recent I-O tables, and interfirm linkages are often difficult to observe. Of available I-O tables (or other sorts of data that can be used to construct I-O tables), some are publicly available, but many (especially for firm-level I-O methods and social accounting matrixes) cost money. The scale of the geography captured in the I-O analysis (and in the associated I-O tables) has complicated implications for accuracy: Analysis of smaller regions might be more accurate in some ways because local I-O tables will more accurately reflect local economic activity and production technology, but more-localized I-O analysis might lose fidelity in the case of supply chains that repeatedly leave and then reenter the region. I-O methods assume that the employed I-O tables provide a census of interlinkages, so inference is not possible without additional models of linkage variation.[16] Relatedly, I-O methods assume

---

[15] Examples of assumptions that have been used to support VAR implementation include assumptions that certain variables do or do not respond within the same period and the direction (sign) of a relationship between variables. Sometimes such assumptions can be justified by economic theory, but sometimes assumptions are justified ad hoc through scenario-specific arguments.

[16] However, some types of uncertainty could be explored ad hoc—for example, by conducting sensitivity analysis around specified linkage value perturbations.

that linkages are static (unchanging) and linear (effects scale linearly regardless of the size of the shock). This assumption will be most accurate for short-run predictions of the effects of relatively small shocks. Accuracy might suffer over longer periods—during which entities will adjust behavior in response to the shock (for example, via input substitution) or otherwise change production technology—and over larger shocks that might induce nonlinear changes.

Requirements and Limitations of Computable General Equilibrium

Like I-O models, CGE models require data for some initial period (potentially from I-O tables) to calibrate the model. But, additionally, CGE models require functions that model production and other economic behaviors and estimates for function parameters. In short, the data and computational requirements of CGE models are very intense. CGE data requirements are at least as intensive for CGE models as they are for I-O models. Moreover, the accuracy of the results of CGE models will be sensitive to each of these elements: accurate calibration data, functional specification, and parameter estimates. Because CGE models are simulation based, confidence intervals can be created for some outputs by simulating the model over a range of values for some parameters, but this cannot practically be done for all permutations of ranges of all parameters. The primary limitation of CGE models—aside from those imposed by the above implementation challenges—is that, because of the equilibrium forecasting nature of the technique, the identification assumptions that allow for a solvable equilibrium in the long run may not be plausible in the short run.

Requirements and Limitations of Panel Regression Models

Finally, turning to PR models, the greatest strength of this class of models begets its most severe limitation. When they can be implemented, PR models provide extremely precise and accurate results and often have a well-supported causal interpretation. The trade-off is that the results often lack external validity and might not be applicable to other instances. Each type of PR model has its own assumptions and data requirements that must be met and often has a proscribed set of specification tests and robustness tests. Most critically, when models take on a causal interpretation, they must satisfy some *exclusion restriction*—some way of isolating the shock from other system variables in the face of confounding relationships, such as reverse causality. Finding shock measures that satisfy exclusion restrictions can be extremely challenging. Finally, panel models are usually less well suited for producing dynamic forecasts that allow one to see how effects are expected to evolve through successive time periods, since panel methods often do not maintain causal interpretation in the face of serial correlation introduced by multiple time periods. Rather, they tend to estimate effects over a given time frame—though the time frame can vary considerably.

All Four Workhorse Methods Are Hindered by Adaptation and Bad Data

None of the four methods are well suited to identifying changes between shock instances that would undermine the validity of empirical estimates obtained from earlier shock instances. Standard implementation of each of the methods treats all instances of shock occurrence the same. Different methods, such as tests for time series structural breaks, would be needed to determine whether responses to shocks changed over time.

Also, across all four methods, poor data availability and quality erode reliability of analytic outputs. There might be situations in which there are insufficient data to successfully distinguish signal from noise at a high level of confidence. In fact, it might even be challenging to characterize the level of uncertainty of estimates, thereby limiting their value for informing decisions.

Conclusion: The Workhorse Empirical Methods Do Not Overcome the Technical Obstacles to Achieving the Analytic Capability Requirements in All Applied Environments

Taken as a whole, the requirements and limitations of the four workhorse methods suggest that they cannot always overcome the technical challenges to achieving the analytic capability requirements. Data availability and quality might not always support method implementation, markets and economies might not operate in ways that are consistent with the assumptions underlying model validity, and adaptation or other changes that occur between shock instances might invalidate findings based on historical data.

One important question is whether this finding extends beyond just the four workhorse empirical methodologies. Would some combination of all existing empirical methodologies, not just the workhorse methodologies, be able to overcome the technical obstacles in a significantly wider array of applied environments? Based on our approach to selecting the four workhorse methodologies, we argue that this finding would, indeed, apply to the universe of available methodologies. We focused on the workhorse models because they are the most widely used, and our analysis suggests that they are most widely used because they typically achieve the best empirical performance relative to the technical challenges identified in Chapter Two, despite their limitations.

Ancillary Finding: The Selection, Construction, and Calibration of an Empirical Analytic Approach Depends on the Context of the Applied Environment, Precluding Plug-and-Play Analyses

The requirements and limitations of the workhorse empirical methods have another implication for the development of an analytic capability to support shock management: Empirical analysis must be tailored to each environment in which analysis is applied. The delicacy of empirical approach design generally precludes plug-and-play analyses that might reliably achieve an analytic capability requirement across all situations in which analysis is desired.

Figure 3.2 depicts a sequence of steps representing the process of designing data analysis for a given situation. An empirical model is the mathematical structure through which data analysis is conducted. The first step of designing the empirical model is evaluating available data, since data availability, completeness, and reliability determine feasible options for each of the remaining steps. The second step, empirical model selection, entails choosing between modeling approaches, such as the choice between VAR, I-O, CGE, or PR for a particular analytic effort. The third step, empirical model construction, is determining model elements, such as shock variable construction, outcome variable construction, covariate inclusion, and the selection of the mathematical function representing the relationship between the shock and outcome variables. The final step is empirical model calibration. In many types of data analysis, some model input variables will have to be estimated from available data, because they will not be avail-

FIGURE 3.2

Context-Specific Factors Drive Design of Empirical Analysis in Several Ways

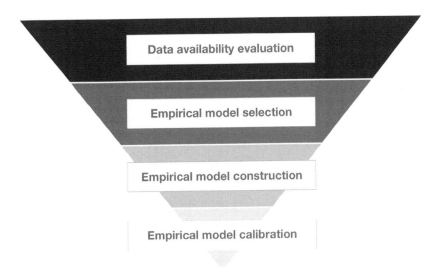

able from direct measurement. This process of determining how to estimate unobserved model inputs is called *calibration*.[17] Progress at the three empirical model design steps requires the careful consideration of factors that typically will vary across the many different environments in which analysis might be desired.

Example of the Context Dependence of Empirical Model Selection

If an analytic question focuses on spillovers, the choice between I-O and CGE modeling approaches will depend on the time frame relevant for the decision under consideration. I-O models will generally be more appropriate if decisionmakers need to understand the immediate effects of a shock,

---

[17] In reality, there is some interaction between stages, so progress through the steps is not perfectly sequential. For instance, the ability of available data to support calibration required for a particular type of model will determine which types of models are feasible to select. Nonetheless, examining each step in isolation simplifies the discussion that follows.

whereas CGE models will generally be more appropriate if decisionmakers are more interested in longer-run shock consequences.

Examples of the Context Dependence of Empirical Model Construction

The choice of how to mathematically define the shock variable can be context dependent. For instance, if the analysis is investigating the contribution of labor costs to the changing geographical concentration of production (a question at the heart of several vignettes), perhaps changes in price are an appropriate shock definition. In contrast, changes in price volatility might be appropriate if the analysis is focusing on the contribution of capital markets to the same changes in production geography.

Similarly, the construction of the outcome variable can be context dependent. For instance, in constructing an empirical model for the vignette on COVID-19 DIB disruptions—e.g., Australian shipbuilding (2020), price might be irrelevant to the immediate consequences of the shock, because, in many cases, no price increase could have alleviated the supply disruption. In contrast, price might be a central outcome of concern in constructing an empirical model for the vignette on cornered markets—i.e., critical materials (circa 2010), since critical materials could be produced elsewhere in the world, but at greater costs.

The underlying mechanism of effect might also drive model structure. For instance, in constructing models for the vignettes on U.S. sanctions on Iran (2011–2020) and the effects of the energy price drop on Russia (2014–2016), the recent history of similar shocks might affect model structure. Russia was able to draw on its National Reserve Fund to cushion spending against shock-induced revenue disruptions. However, this means that Russia has less of a cushion available for future shocks unless it prioritizes rebuilding the fund. Therefore, models of subsequent shocks on Russia might incorporate variables reflecting the recent history of shocks since that history might dramatically affect shock consequences.

Example of the Context Dependence of Empirical Model Calibration

Model calibration can depend on the context of the situation being analyzed. For example, consider a situation in which an I-O model is being employed to estimate spillovers stemming from an industry-level shock, but the I-O table for the nation being analyzed is several years out of date. A current I-O table from another region might be used to estimate an updated I-O table for the nation being analyzed, but the choice of nation to base the update on depends on the nature of the economy being analyzed. An I-O table from an industrialized nation would be a poor choice for calibration of a model analyzing the effects of a shock on the economic sectors in an agrarian nation.

Finding 5: (Gap) Even If the Technical Obstacles to Achieving the Analytic Capability Requirements in All Applied Environments Were Overcome, Additional Analysis Would Be Needed to Leverage These Empirical Insights to Inform Decisionmaking

Our analysis of the vignettes suggests that the technical challenges to obtaining precise, accurate, and reliable empirical outputs are not the only obstacles to providing analytic support to defense decisionmakers. Aside from the question of how to best conduct empirical analyses, two additional questions arose frequently during our analysis of the vignettes:

1. What empirical analyses should be conducted? That is, what hypotheses should data analyses test?
2. What do the outputs of empirical analyses suggest about the COAs under consideration?

We found that additional analysis is needed to address these two questions. We next describe each of these gaps in turn. In the next chapter, we propose that these gaps can be reduced through the construction of tailored frameworks consisting of interrelated models of pertinent aspects of shock initiation, propagation, and impact.

Insufficient Foundational Understanding of Shock Mechanisms to Specify Empirical Analyses

For several of the analytic capability requirements presented in Chapter Two, we determined that there was insufficient understanding of the mechanisms underlying shock instigation, propagation, and effects to propose empirical analyses. Tables 2.4–2.7 listed analytic capability requirements and associated analytic questions for each of the management foci. Several entries do not contain questions but instead include a note that more foundational analysis is needed. These analytic capability requirements are as follows (with associated management focus in parentheses):

- **understanding shock instigation (all management foci).** This capability supports the detection and anticipation of a shock—for example, by suggesting where sensing and analytic efforts should be focused and what indicators to look for. Empirical analysis to achieve this might entail testing where in economies and markets and under what conditions events occur and translate into shocks. However, preliminary analysis is needed to propose what types of events to analyze, what markets and economies to examine, and what conditions to consider.
- **identifying points of potential intervention (all management foci).** This capability supports the assessment of potential management approaches. A precursor to assessing the potential cost-effectiveness of interventions is proposing what factors might affect shock occurrence and consequences in the desired manner and identifying which of those factors are subject to influence.
- **assessing alternative forms of supply or production (supply restriction).** Such an assessment might entail empirical estimation of the feasibility and cost-effectiveness of accessing alternative supply or production resources. But preliminary analysis is needed—for example, to identify potential constraints and enablers to feasibility and to identify the types of costs associated with sources of supply (for instance, are there political or other nonfinancial costs to consider?).
- **connecting inferred priorities to government strategy, intent, or constraints (inference of government priorities).** Straightforward empirical analysis might be sufficient to describe the response of government fiscal policy to an economic shock affecting its fiscal position, but inferring government priorities from that observation requires additional analysis. For instance, foundational analysis of government political and economic constraints might be needed to propose an empirical approach to testing whether the government response to the shock is driven by internal constraints or strategic objectives.
- **estimating the risk of some particular extreme response to a shock (extreme response).** Decisionmakers might find it helpful to have a

sense of not only whether and under what conditions victims of an economic shock might resort to an extreme response but also—more dauntingly—which extreme response might occur. An initial approach to assessing the risk of any extreme response occurring might entail examining conditions of the economy and evaluating people's economic well-being. In contrast, it is unclear what empirical approach might support analysis of whether and under what conditions the extreme response will take the form of, say, external military aggression versus regime change. Substantial foundational work is needed to improve understanding of what drives the various types of extreme response in order to propose empirical analysis to achieve this analytic capability requirement.

Lack of an Approach for Connecting Empirical Outputs and Potential Courses of Action

A distinct challenge from obtaining precise, accurate, and reliable empirical outputs is knowing what to do with those outputs. For instance, Chapter Five presents a case study in which several of the workhorse methods are employed to explore how empirical analysis could support the consideration and design of U.S. sanctions on Iran. I-O analysis presented in this chapter identifies economic sectors to which aggregate economic conditions are most sensitive (that is, which sectors should be sanctioned if the objective is to cause the greatest decline in overall economic output). One VAR analysis presented in this chapter finds that the economic effects of sanctions on oil—one of the sectors identified in the I-O analysis—would dissipate over time as the economy adapts. Another VAR analysis finds that sanctions on oil are likely to cause a more-substantial decline in defense spending than other types of government spending.

Although these empirical outputs provide information that seems useful to decisionmakers, questions remain about how to interpret this information in the context of the policy decisions under consideration. Will the decline in Iranian defense spending translate into delayed achievement of nuclear weapons capability? Do sanctions cause a level of collateral damage in the Iranian economy or to Iran's trade partners that is severe enough to be an unacceptable cost of imposing sanctions? Empirical analysis alone cannot guide decisionmakers in answering such questions.

CHAPTER FOUR

Frameworks to Enhance Analytic Support to Defense Decisionmakers

Chapter Three described several gaps between what can be achieved with existing empirical methods and what capabilities are required for leveraging available data to support defense decisionmakers responsible for managing the consequences of economic shocks. In that chapter, we argued that closing some of the gaps calls for a capability to incorporate into analyses key aspects of the mechanisms underlying the instigation, propagation, and effects of shocks.

In this chapter, we describe our proposed approach: building for each applied environment an overarching construct, which we term a *framework,* that models decision-relevant mechanisms affecting shock instigation, propagation, and effects. The main objective of a framework is to connect analytic outputs to the COAs under consideration for managing shock consequences. We argue that, on the way to achieving this main objective, a framework can also help fill the other gaps identified in Chapter Three: specifying the empirical analyses needed to achieve analytic capability requirements and overcoming the technical challenges to high-quality empirical results.

In this chapter, we describe the concept of a framework in more detail. First, we explain how a framework might fill the gaps identified in Chapter Three. Second, we draw on the vignettes to identify several features of the applied environment that a framework should be able to incorporate. Third, we introduce a preliminary and partial framework for shock-induced supply restrictions.

How Frameworks Improve Data-Informed Management of the Consequences of Economic Shocks

Frameworks as Facilitators of the Orientation Phase of an Observe, Orient, Decide, Act Loop

A gap identified in Chapter Three was support for connecting analytic outputs to COAs under consideration. Filling this gap is the primary objective of this framework. Empirical analysis can uncover information about how a system operates. Ideally, empirical outputs accurately describe the effects of the shock on outcomes of interest under various COA counterfactuals. But, as with any type of empirical analysis, these outputs alone do not identify the best management choice. As we envision them, frameworks are designed to help decisionmakers translate empirical outputs into insight about the implications of alternative COAs for decisionmaker objectives.

One way to view this function of a framework is as a facilitator of the orientation phase of an OODA loop representing the process of managing the consequences of an economic shock. Figure 4.1 illustrates this process. The empirical analysis that is the focus of this study is part of the "observe" phase, and the management decision or policy that the analysis supports is the "decide" phase.

One point of reference supporting the potential value and concept of frameworks connecting analytic output to decisions is comparison with how economists use the above methods to inform macroeconomic policy. The workhorse empirical methods described in Chapter Three were developed by economists to answer specific questions about the economic consequences of shocks. Yet economic policymaking entities combine these empirical methods with other modeling approaches that help them to evaluate the consequences of policies under consideration against their ultimate objectives—for example, by helping them to balance trade-offs between different dimensions of well-being.

Put differently, *even in the discipline that has put the most effort into studying shocks, economists need frameworks to leverage the output of workhorse empirical methods to inform actual policy decisions.*

FIGURE 4.1

Frameworks Structure the Orientation Phase of an Observe, Orient, Decide, Act Loop

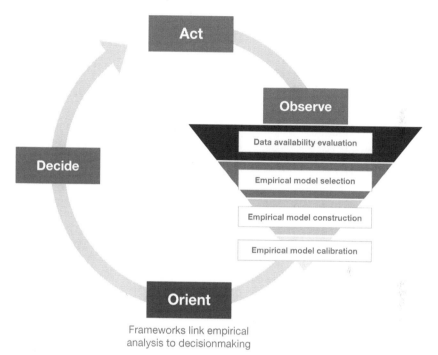

Frameworks link empirical
analysis to decisionmaking

How Frameworks Can Help Identify What Analyses Are Needed

Another of the gaps identified in Chapter Three is the need for better understanding of the mechanisms underlying shock instigation, propagation, and effects to propose empirically testable hypotheses. Frameworks hypothesize models of selected shock mechanisms. In some cases, aspects of these frameworks might focus on mechanisms that are the subject of an analytic capability requirement. Here, we provide an example by discussing how frameworks might facilitate the formulation of analysis questions for an analytic capability requirement identified in Chapter Three as needing more foundational work: connecting inferred priorities to government strategy, intent, or constraints.

As a notional example, suppose that empirical analysis shows that a government cut its spending in the wake of a shock, rather than increasing revenue through taxes. A subsequent question is what this observed prioritization reveals about government strategy, intent, or constraints. For instance, did the government choose not to raise taxes because it was more willing to forgo public expenditure than to raise taxes on certain types of transactions, perhaps for political reasons?

Economic theory suggests an alternative explanation: Perhaps the government could not raise taxes because of fundamental economic dynamics. Increasing a tax rate can reduce the number of market transactions, thereby reducing the tax base. Consequently, there are situations in which increasing tax rate can reduce tax revenue. This dynamic can mean that the government in question cut spending because it was not economically feasible to increase revenue—not that the government was protecting a market from the burden of higher tax rates.

A framework incorporating a model of these market dynamics could point to testable hypotheses to help distinguish between these two scenarios. In this case, such a model might pose testable hypotheses about an economic quantity called the *price elasticity of demand,* which quantifies the ease with which consumers can reduce spending on a good or service when its price increases. Empirical studies of price elasticity might reveal whether raising taxes was a feasible option for raising revenue, improving the accuracy of inference about the implications of the government's response.

Frameworks Can Help Overcome the Technical Obstacles to Achieving the Analytic Capability Requirements

A third gap identified in Chapter Three was the inability of existing workhorse methods to always overcome the technical obstacles to high-quality empirical outputs. In some cases, a framework might help overcome binding technical obstacles—for instance, by sidestepping or minimizing limitations imposed by bad data. One way it might do so is by explicitly modeling adaptation and attrition that might follow past shocks and thereby specifying hypotheses to help test for adaptation and attrition and account for them in the overall analysis.

Another way a framework might minimize limitations imposed by bad data is by focusing empirical analysis on ranges of the feature space in which the choice between management alternatives hinges on analytic results. Efforts in the design and execution of empirical analysis can then focus on those decision boundaries, potentially reducing the performance requirements of the methods in terms of achieving precision across the entire range of possible analytic outputs.

For instance, the level of precision that an empirical analysis must achieve to be useful for decisionmakers might vary with the decisions under consideration. Suppose that decisionmakers are considering investing in workforce development to promote growth of a DIB. If the investment decision entails deciding whether to spend $20,000 per worker to train a 1,000-person workforce, analysis must determine whether the total net benefit exceeds the $20 million investment. In contrast, if the investment decision is how many workers to train at a cost of $20,000 per worker, then both the analytic question and required precision are different. Here, the analysis must identify the number of workers for whom the training's marginal value exceeds $20,000 per person. Such a calculation will require reliable estimates for several decision-relevant parameters.

A framework clearly delineating the relationship between analytic outputs and decision thresholds can help reduce unnecessary analytic complexity and data burden—for example, by avoiding the second, more-complex type of workforce training analysis, if the simpler first analysis discriminates sufficiently well between the investment choices under consideration.

Figure 4.2 illustrates how this concept might apply across all steps of empirical analysis design. A framework can support iteration and coordination between each step of the design process by appealing to the mechanism underlying shock instigation, propagation, and effects to identify the overlap between minimal requirements to inform decisionmaking and the most feasible execution approach.

FIGURE 4.2

Frameworks Can Enhance the Congruity of Empirical Analysis with the Specific Context, Helping to Overcome Technical Challenges to Reliable Empirical Outputs

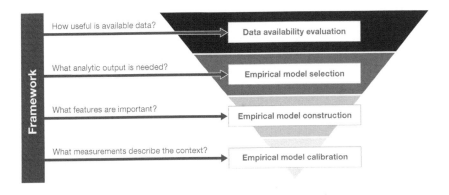

Features That a Framework Might Take into Account

Through analyzing the vignettes, we identified several characteristics that frameworks would ideally incorporate.

Leverage Modular Framework Structure to Balance the Benefits of Tailoring Analysis to Each Applied Environment with the Benefits of Aggregating Information Across Environments

A challenge of analyzing shocks is that while there are similarities across shock instances, there are also differences, and it can be difficult to design analyses that are flexible enough to account for both. Consider three vignettes featuring reductions in government budgets: U.S. sanctions on Iran (2011–2020), the U.S. Budget Control Act (2013), and the effects of the energy price drop on Russia (2014–2016). An analysis trying to infer government priorities from the government's response to the budget reductions might benefit from exploiting similarities in the three applied environments, as long as the analysis also accounts for important differences.

As discussed earlier, inferring government priorities might require exploring the latitude governments had to raise revenue by increasing taxes. To the extent that some markets might be similar in Iran, Russia, and the United States, analytic methods and results in one of these applied environments might also be applicable in the other two environments. For example, because many commodities and consumer goods are traded in common global markets, it might be possible to save analysts time by using the same approach in all three environments. Or perhaps price elasticity of demand could be more precisely measured by pooling data across the three environments, if there is good reason to suspect that elasticities for some goods are about the same in all three countries.

Yet frameworks for these three applied environments might diverge in other ways. Inferring government priorities might also require exploring the consequences of reducing different types of government spending. Government spending program structures and population needs might differ substantially across Iran, Russia, and the United States, so it seems likely that this analysis must be tailored to each country in order to be valid.

We propose that modular framework architecture could help balance the need for analysis tailored to each applied environment with the benefits of aggregating information across environments. Each module would capture a specific aspect of the mechanism of shock instigation, propagation, and effect. The exact modular composition of a framework would vary from one situation to the next, depending on details of the applied environment, such as the nature of the economic shock, the consequences with which decisionmakers are concerned, COAs under consideration, economic features, and political institutions.

Account for Potential Path Dependence

An important, but potentially subtle, feature of shocks is that they can fundamentally change the economies, markets, or supply chains that they affect. Consequently, frameworks intended to anticipate the consequences of shocks should account for the historical sequence of shocks, and not just the specific shock instance under consideration.

Shocks can have lasting effects in several ways:

1. **Adaptation:** Decisionmakers in economies, markets, or supply chains affected by a shock might change their behavior in response to that shock, adapting so that subsequent occurrences of the same type of event do not have such severe consequences.

2. **Selection:** A shock might favor or disfavor certain types of institutions, firms, individuals, or other entities, changing the composition of relevant market structures and, therefore, the consequences of future shock events.

3. **Attrition:** On the other hand, a shock might deplete resources available to avoid, recover from, or otherwise mitigate the adverse consequences of future shock, increasing susceptibility to damage from future occurrences of the same type of event.

The vignettes provide several examples of such path dependence. The vignette on the effects of the energy price drop on Russia (2014–2016) offers an example of attrition. A single, temporary drop in energy prices would not have had especially severe consequences for Russia because Russia anticipated the potential for abrupt changes in energy prices and created a reserve fund to mitigate resulting budgetary pressure. Russia sustained meaningful damage as a result of energy price drops from 2014 to 2016 because there were repeated bouts of price drops with insufficient time in between bouts for Russia to rebuild the reserve fund. A framework for examining the effects of energy price drops on Russia would likely be most accurate if it accounted for the recent history of shocks to account for the attrition of the reserve fund.

Account for the Role of Uncertainty in Allocation Decisions

How decisionmakers in economies, markets, and supply chains account for uncertainty can have important implications for the consequences of shocks and, therefore, might be important to incorporate into frameworks. Decisionmaker response to uncertainty is central to shock consequences in several vignettes in which the geographic concentration of production rendered supply chains vulnerable to disruption.

In the two vignettes on the U.S. rubber supply (WWII), and the German oil supply (WWII), prewar geographic concentration of production was a latent vulnerability that was later exploited by each country's adversaries. But if events had gone differently—if the United States had not been drawn into war with Japan, or if the war had ended quickly, as many in German leadership had assumed—the geographic concentration of production might never have been a problem. Under these counterfactuals, investment in alternative sources of supply would have seemed wasteful. In contrast, if leaders in the United States and Germany had invested more resources earlier into avoiding or mitigating the consequences of geographically concentrated production of these critical materials, they might have suffered less from shortages, and a proactive response might have been less expensive than the reactive response both countries ultimately took. In both vignettes, what history would deem the "best" decision hinged critically on factors that decisionmakers could not have known with certainty in advance. Therefore, decisionmaker response to uncertainty was pivotal. In both of these vignettes, decisionmakers chose to accept some risk of geographically concentrated production, which later had significant consequences for the course of the war.

In a similar vein, economic shocks that cause program delays and loss of sources of supply might be fairly benign if no unexpected mobilizations occur but might be damaging or even catastrophic if they do precede or coincide with an unexpected mobilization. The vignette on COVID-19 DIB disruptions—e.g., Australian shipbuilding (2020) offers a modern variation of the decisions that pre-WWII leaders faced. As of the time of this writing (mid-2021), the COVID-19 pandemic appears to have delayed Australian shipbuilding efforts, yet this delay does not appear to have significantly compromised Australian military objectives. The resources Australia should invest in to mitigate the effects of the delay depend on decisionmakers' beliefs about the probability that the program delay will have military consequences in the future.

As these examples illustrate, uncertainty can complicate management of the consequences of economic shocks. If there is a possibility that the shock will not cause severe damage—for example, because the risk of future conflict or mobilization is low—it might be hard to justify directing resources toward its mitigation. Similarly, where the adverse consequences of a shock are far in the future, in the absence of an exigent need for action, decision-makers might simply bet on having time to respond if needed.[1] Frameworks might need to explicitly account for decisionmaker response to such uncertainty.

A Preliminary and Partial Framework for Shock-Induced Supply Restriction

The supply restriction management focus is particularly important for defense decisionmakers, and it is one to which we devoted significant attention. Supply restriction is the central outcome of most of the vignettes. This management focus encompasses the initial motivation for this project, discussed in Chapter One: that economic shocks might have the same consequences as kinetic supply interdiction. Consistently with the importance of this concern, ongoing DoD and congressional lines of effort to improve management of supply chain risk typically seek to reduce risk of supply restrictions. Finally, shock-induced supply restriction occurs through complex mechanisms, providing a rich setting in which to further explore approaches to leveraging frameworks to improve empirical analysis.

The Need for a Supply Restriction Framework

The comparison of two vignettes featuring supply restriction helps illustrate the value that a framework can provide. Supply restriction in the vignettes on U.S. access to Russian RD-180 engines (circa 2014) and British shipbuilding (circa 1980s) threatened defense postures in different ways, and potential mitigations were correspondingly different:

---

[1] These factors of deciding not to act because of uncertainty about the likelihood, severity, or timing of economic shocks have had crippling effects in the civilian sector. For example, the absence of perceived immediate need for investment in the construction of new floodwater protections in Louisiana ultimately led to extensive disruption to the state's economy in the aftermath of Hurricane Katrina. For more, see Sheri Lee Fink, *Five Days at Memorial: Life and Death in a Storm-Ravaged Hospital*, New York: Crown Publishers, 2013.

- **The time horizon of shock effects:** The United States losing access to Russian RD-180 motors could have threatened ongoing U.S. military space operations by inhibiting the U.S. military's ability to launch new satellites. In contrast, the erosion of British shipbuilding capability and capacity during the 1980s might not have impacted ongoing operations. However, over a longer time horizon, the loss of the shipbuilding industry could have compromised fleet modernization goals, potentially degrading future military capabilities.
- **Appropriate COAs to mitigate shock effects:** A COA to mitigate damage from the potential loss of space launch capability would need to ensure (or obviate the need for) supply immediately. Since production capability and capacity take time to build, appropriate COAs entail accessing existing sources of supply. In contrast, the long horizon before the potential military consequences of eroded British shipbuilding made COAs that required longer implementation time feasible. However, the long horizon posed other challenges, such as policy instability stemming from changes in political leadership, which ultimately undermined successful policy implementation.

The core task of empirical analysis is to examine the relationship between shock outcomes and features of the shock and the applied environment. Given the difference in time horizons, outcomes of interest, and features underpinning potential COAs, it follows that these two vignettes call for different empirical approaches. Empirical analyses for each vignette would need to test different sets of hypotheses, the mathematical relationships between shock outcomes and features of the shock and applied environment might differ, and calibration of even the same model parameter might differ given the economic changes that might occur over such long horizons.

With the benefit of hindsight, we can identify important distinctions between these two vignettes with relative ease. Making such distinctions for novel and ongoing situations might not be so easy. Yet we propose that the concept of a framework offers a unified approach to designing appropriate empirical analyses even across diverse emerging supply restriction scenarios, such as these two vignettes might have presented to decisionmakers as they were occurring.

The first task to building such a framework is addressing the following question: How can the diverse range of supply restriction scenarios be partitioned—using information available as the scenarios are occurring—into distinct groups such that the scenarios in each group can be approached with similar types of analysis?

The Hierarchical Structure of a Supply Restriction Framework

We propose a hierarchical structure of supply restriction frameworks, where the top-level module partitions supply restrictions based on features that determine appropriate analytic approaches. Lower-level modules then help structure analyses, depending on the concerns of the decisionmakers and features of the supply restriction scenario.

A Top-Level Module That Uses Shock Latency as a Heuristic for Selecting Lower-Level Modules

In Chapter One, we introduced a model whereby the consequences of a shock depend on the outcome of a race between shock propagation and the response of shocked entities. For a shock of a given latency,[2] the faster decisionmakers can proceed through OODA loops to effectively respond to a shock and thereby avoid or mitigate damage, the less damage the shock will cause.

Furthermore, features of the DIB production process, such as those listed in Figure 4.3, mediate the speed of both shock propagation and the response of the shocked entity. Production time is the duration of the production process. Supply chain topology is the number of firms at each layer in the supply chain and the extent of connectivity across layers. Supply chain geography refers to the spatial location of each source in a supply chain. Supply chain stability refers to the extent of firm entry and exit at each layer in the supply chain. We propose that the exposure to shocks, the way shocks prop-

---

[2] In many situations, shock duration is also central to the amount of damage caused, particularly because the shocked entity might not detect the shock and therefore might not be able to respond until it starts suffering the effects of the shock. However, to simplify preliminary model presentation, we focus on shock latency.

FIGURE 4.3

Time-Oriented Model of Shock Features, Production Process Characteristics, and Response and Adaptation Behavior of the Shocked Entities

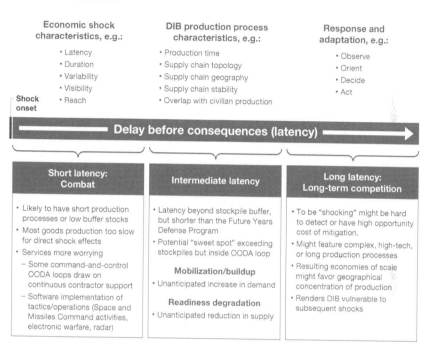

Economic shock characteristics, e.g.:
- Latency
- Duration
- Variability
- Visibility
- Reach

DIB production process characteristics, e.g.:
- Production time
- Supply chain topology
- Supply chain geography
- Supply chain stability
- Overlap with civilian production

Response and adaptation, e.g.:
- Observe
- Orient
- Decide
- Act

Shock onset

Delay before consequences (latency)

Short latency: Combat
- Likely to have short production processes or low buffer stocks
- Most goods production too slow for direct shock effects
- Services more worrying
  - Some command-and-control OODA loops draw on continuous contractor support
  - Software implementation of tactics/operations (Space and Missiles Command activities, electronic warfare, radar)

Intermediate latency
- Latency beyond stockpile buffer, but shorter than the Future Years Defense Program
- Potential "sweet spot" exceeding stockpiles but inside OODA loop

Mobilization/buildup
- Unanticipated increase in demand

Readiness degradation
- Unanticipated reduction in supply

Long latency: Long-term competition
- To be "shocking" might be hard to detect or have high opportunity cost of mitigation.
- Might feature complex, high-tech, or long production processes
- Resulting economies of scale might favor geographical concentration of production
- Renders DIB vulnerable to subsequent shocks

agate through supply chains, and resilience or response all hinge on these features. Finally, we propose that market dynamics in response to shocks vary considerably for dual-use and dedicated military use technologies and components.

The model constituting the highest level of the framework partitions supply restriction scenarios into three groups, each of which will form the basis of a lower-level module: Short-latency shocks can potentially affect ongoing combat operations. Long-latency shocks are most relevant in long-term competition, affecting production capabilities and technology. In between these extremes is an intermediate-latency period characterized by shock outcomes that are most sensitive to features of the shock and the applied environment.

Short-Latency Shocks

In the short term, economic shocks can lead to logistical challenges that impede a military's capability to project force. Generally, militaries conduct logistical analysis and stockpile the necessary material to maintain force readiness. However, the costs of doing so always limit the extent of stockpiling. We propose that the types of DIB-supported capabilities most vulnerable to short-latency shocks have short production processes and, consequently, tend to have smaller stockpile buffers since just-in-time production has cost advantages at little loss of responsiveness for quickly produced goods. This requirement for short production processes substantially limits the range of manufactured products that could drive such immediate supply restrictions. However, services on which ongoing operations rely might be more vulnerable to this type of shock consequence. For instance, many military command and control systems rely on essential and ongoing contractor support for such services as software development and implementation.

Long-Latency Shocks

At the other end of the spectrum, in the long term, any economy or DIB could potentially adapt to almost any economic shock. In the United States, the predominant construct driving defense investment choices is the Future Years Defense Program, so we might benchmark U.S. ability to respond to a shock affecting production capability and capacity as, at most, five years. So, if the United States could complete an OODA loop for a shock in five years, what types of shocks would the OODA loop not work well for? We propose that the types of shocks that cause long-term effects must either be hard to detect or have a high opportunity cost of response. If the shock could be detected and if there were low trade-offs associated with mitigating its effects, then the shock would not have the opportunity to cause substantial damage beyond the five-year (in the case of the United States) OODA loop.

These two requirements suggest that the types of DIB-supported capabilities that might be vulnerable to such shocks might have production processes with high fixed costs, perhaps because of their technical sophistication, complexity, large physical system size, or reliance on rare natural resources. Economic theory indicates that high fixed production costs limit firm entry, suggesting that such industries might be very concentrated among a few producers. By similar dynamics, such industries might tend to feature geographical concentration. Working against such economic dynamics might require substantial investment in the form of industrial policy, and such policies might be contrary to other economic interests that favor low production costs and low taxes.

Intermediate-Latency Shocks

In between short- and long-latency shocks, there is an intermediate-latency category. Over a period of time longer than what a stockpile could buffer against but shorter than a nation's OODA loop, we suspect that the outcome of the race between shock propagation and response and adaptation is most "competitive," in the sense that the outcome of the race is most sensitive to variation in the system characteristics, such as those identified in Figure 4.3. In particular, if geopolitical events lead to military buildup or mobilization, a concurrent economic shock might influence, or even decide, conflict outcomes. This might be especially true if adversary nations are less exposed to the shock, more resilient to the shock, or able to more quickly respond because of shorter OODA loops. Similarly, if a country suffers an unanticipated readiness degradation (for example, the discovery of widespread equipment flaws or a relative readiness degradation resulting from adversary technological advances), the country and its DIB will need time to restore readiness, and a shock during this time period could make the nation unexpectedly vulnerable.

Lower-Level Modules for Shocks of Different Latencies

This proposed framework of shock-induced supply restriction points to several features of shocks, capabilities, DIBs, and national institutions that could help defense decisionmakers and supporting analysts classify shock instances they face into one of three lower-level modules for analysis: short latency, long latency, and intermediate latency.[3] We anticipate that appro-

---

[3] There might also be cases in which the same shock has different latencies in different markets, in which case analysts and decisionmakers might find value in applying multiple lower-level modules to examine shock consequences across different horizons. There might be additional value in the development of a third module that synthesizes the findings of these modules to support decisionmakers' evaluation of the trade-offs between COA consequences at different horizons.

priate analytic questions and methods will vary across these three modules. Table 4.1 summarizes potential differences in analytic approaches, as reflected in different consideration modules for short- and long-latency shock.

Short-Latency Shocks

Response to short-latency shocks entails whether, how, and to what extent to find alternative sources of supply (potentially including foreign and domestic sources), to find alternative sources of military capability (for instance, substituting less-preferred weapon systems), or to forgo the military capability and mitigate the operational consequences. This decision space might lead to several submodules that will discipline subsequent empirical analysis. A module describing the factors driving speed, achievable scale, and cost of quickly increasing existing production capacity might trigger different empirical analyses than a module describing factors driving the speed, achievable scale, and cost of building new production capacity and recruiting civilian production resources into DIB supply chains (that is, mobilization). To support decisions about finding alternative sources of military capability, a submodule examining doctrinal employment of different weapon systems might be helpful.

Long-Latency Shocks

For long-latency shocks, the decision space looks quite different, focusing on what types of investment could preserve or create production capacity and capability and on the appropriate level of investment given the risk of future damage from supply restrictions that might occur without such investment. Assessing the risk of disruption might require a submodule connecting status quo production patterns to disruption risk. Developing and evaluating investment options might require empirical analyses of the drivers of industrial capability and capacity and of the costs and benefits of various types of industrial policy.

TABLE 4.1

Proposed Analytic Considerations for Short- and Long-Latency Shocks

Shock Latency	Decision Space	Module Considerations
Short-latency shocks	Whether and how to find alternative supply	Surge module to assess mitigation value of existing production capacity
	Whether and how to find alternative military capability	Mobilization module to assess mitigation value of recruiting civilian production capacity
	How to mitigate loss of supply and/or capability	Doctrinal module to assess feasibility, costs, and benefits of employing alternative military capability
Long-latency shocks	What level of investment does the risk justify?	Disruption risk module to assess supply risk associated with global production and trade patterns
	What types of investment in production capacity and capability are needed?	Industrial capability and capacity module to identify drivers of development and decline of localized industrial activity
		Industrial policy module to evaluate how policy choices mitigate risk

CHAPTER FIVE

A Case Study of Historical Sanctions Against Iran

Our examination of the vignettes described earlier highlighted commonality in both the challenges that economic shocks pose to the DIB and defense operations and the types of questions that economic methodology should be able to address in order to be of most use to decisionmakers. We conducted a review of the economic literature to identify the leading empirical methods used to examine related events in academic research and identified four approaches that have been applied across a wide range of shocks, consequences of interest, and time horizons: I-O, VAR, CGE, and PR models.

In this chapter, we apply several of these methods to analyze one vignette offering a recent example of an economic shock with DIB implications: U.S. sanctions on Iran (2011–2020). We selected this vignette for further consideration here in part because all three management foci are at play, as depicted in Table 2.3. There, we noted that the case of Iran sanctions offers a testbed to explore empirical analyses of the effects of supply restriction, the potential for extreme reactions from a nation placed under sanction, and the possibility of eliciting a nation's spending priorities. Rather than focusing on a high-fidelity policy analysis here, our examination of this case study serves to illustrate more concretely how the methods operate, the outputs they produce, the insights they provide, and their challenges and shortcomings. While we demonstrate the above against a specific backdrop, these observations apply to a large number of other cases of interest.

Background

The United States has levied various sanctions against Iran since the Iran hostage crisis following the takeover of the U.S. embassy in Tehran in 1979.[1] We focus in particular on the effects of sanctions that occurred after the 2015 JCPOA. These have occurred in several waves, such as the 2017 Countering America's Adversaries Through Sanctions Act and the reimposition of pre-JCPOA sanctions in 2018. More recently, retaliatory sanctions were placed on Iran following the attacks on U.S. forces that took place in response to the killing of Qasem Soleimani in 2020. Additional sanctions have followed and remain in place as of the time of writing this report (mid-2021). While sanctions have been applied to numerous sectors (e.g., energy, shipping, banking, construction, mining, textiles, manufacturing, and metals), they have historically focused on the oil industry, which is a significant driver of the Iranian economy. For this reason, we largely model how sanctions to Iran's oil industry affect production in the Iranian economy, though in one segment of the analysis we consider how shocks affect production in each individual sector of the economy.

Analytic Capability Requirements to Support U.S. Decisionmakers

U.S. policymakers responsible for deciding whether and how to impose sanctions might find value in many types of analysis. Here, we focus on the specific decision of which sectors of the Iranian economy the United States should sanction in order to delay Iran's achievement of an operational nuclear weapons capability.[2] Our primary goal is to illustrate how a suite of economic methods can be used for decision support. We examine two

---

[1] There have also been multilateral sanctions levied against Iran, particularly those issued by the United States, the European Union, and the UN beginning in 2006.

[2] To simplify the exposition of this chapter, we did not consider the related question of whether sanctions are the best way to achieve U.S. objectives or precursor questions, such as how to measure the achievement of U.S. objectives. Our objective is not to offer a full analysis of U.S. sanctions on Iran but instead to illustrate application of the work-horse empirical methods, their value, and their limitations.

key dimensions of interest: (1) the benefits of various sanctions packages in terms of their effectiveness in delaying Iran's achievement of nuclear weapons capability and (2) the costs of those packages, including their collateral damage—the damage they impose that does not directly contribute to the U.S. objective of delayed nuclear capability. Below, we examine the extent to which workhorse economic methods are able to inform these quantities of interest, and we identify where gaps in the analysis remain.

How to estimate the benefits and costs of sanctions packages depends on the mechanism underlying sanction effects. In this chapter, we envision two potential mechanisms. First, sanctions might cause a deterioration of Iran's overall economy, resulting in political pressure on the Iranian government to comply with U.S. demands so that sanctions are removed. Second, sanctions might deprive the Iranian government of the funds needed to pursue nuclear weapon R&D by reducing tax revenue and increasing government spending on economic support in affected economic sectors and to households.

The first two rows of Table 5.1 identify two analytic capability requirements for estimating the effectiveness of various sanctions packages through these mechanisms. To address the first analytic capability requirement—identifying exposure to and predicting military consequences of a shock—we measure how sanctions affect relevant national-level outcomes, such as Iran's overall economy, government spending on various programs (including military spending), and political trends. The second analytic capability requirement is to estimate how proposed sanctions on one sector of the economy affect other sectors. This analysis might inform sanctions package effectiveness, as well as undesirable collateral damage that does not help achieve U.S. objectives.

Sanctions might cause many other types of collateral damage. For the empirical analysis presented in this chapter, we focus on the question of how sanctions packages are likely to affect other key nations—be they allies, partners, or adversaries. The third row of Table 5.1 specifies the analytic capability requirement for estimating this type of collateral damage.

TABLE 5.1

The Case Study Illustrates How a Suite of Economic Methods Can Be Used for Decision Support by Illustrating Their Achievement of Three Key Analytic Capability Requirements

Analytic Capability Requirement	Analysis Questions	Analytic Method
Identifying exposure to and predicting military consequences of a shock	How connected are DIBs to markets exposed to the shock, and with what level of sensitivity?	VAR
Predicting and detecting ripple effects of shocks to other economic sectors	How connected are other sectors to shocked industries, and with what level of sensitivity?	I-O
Predicting and detecting ripple effects of shocks to trading partners	How connected are other countries' economies to shocked industries, and with what level of sensitivity?	International trade analysis

How We Applied Economic Methodology to the Case Study

In this section, we describe how we employed the methods described in Chapter Three to the present case study. Of the four methods we discussed, the case study focuses on VARs and I-O analysis because of their relevance to the context and the availability of public data to support them. CGE modeling would provide valuable analysis; it is especially well suited for examining international trade ramifications. We did not build a CGE model to support the case study because of the lack of sufficiently detailed publicly available data and the relative costs and benefits of the approach in relation to the goals of the case study. Instead, we analyzed product-level trade flows to highlight the role played by the international dimension in the broader analysis and to provide a sense of the outputs that would stem from this type of modeling. PR models are less well suited to this particular case study but could be of use in similar contexts that ask a different set of research questions. Table 5.1 associates each analytic method described below with the analytic capability requirements targeted by this case study.

Importantly, each modeling approach is accompanied by a set of assumptions that influences the outputs it produces. A decisionmaker can thus focus on the results produced by methods for which the underlying assumptions are appropriate to the context and understand the role that assumptions play in comparing potential COAs. Ultimately, the decision-maker should have a sense of how shocks contribute to the success of mission objectives, and at what cost, by changing key variables.

Vector Autoregression Models

VARs are dynamic forecasting models that can both estimate shocks and project their effects over time. VARs and I-O analysis complement each other in a number of ways. For example, while both approaches are capable of estimating the effects of a shock on GDP, VARs are able to more precisely capture how the effects are expected to unfold over time. Moreover, while I-O models are inherently production-centric, VARs are able to estimate effects on a host of economic, military, and political variables, such as capital formation, trade, military spending, and levels of democracy. These capabilities pair nicely with the more sector- and firm-focused I-O models, helping to drive toward a better understanding of how key outcomes are likely to be affected. For example, forecasts of the effect of a shock on military spending versus other types of government spending help illustrate the trade-offs that the government may be forced to consider in response to falling revenue. Estimates of political variables, such as the level of democracy or regime change, can provide a sense of the pressure that may be placed on the governing regime along a different dimension.

Our VAR specifications are based on leading papers in the sanctions literature.[3] We followed the literature in operationalizing sanctions through a negative shock to oil and gas rents, where *rents* are defined as the value of production (at world prices) minus the total costs of production. As discussed earlier, while sanctions have been placed on numerous sectors of the Iranian economy, they have primarily targeted the oil sector. We used a series of VAR models to estimate the causal effect of a shock to oil and gas rents on a host of variables that may be of interest to policymakers over the following five years. Specifically, we studied how sanctions affect Iran's

---

[3] See, for instance, Mohammad R. Farzanegan, "Oil Revenue Shocks and Government Spending Behavior in Iran," *Energy Economics*, Vol. 33, No. 6, 2011; Dizaji and Van Bergeijk, 2013; and Dizaji and Farzanegan, 2019.

GDP, military spending, nonmilitary government spending, imports, gross capital formation, the polity score, and other disaggregated categories of government spending.[4] Polity scores measure levels of democracy and are described further in Appendix C.

The key assumption that allows us to identify the causal effect of the shock is that oil and gas rents do not respond to movements in the other variables within the same year. This assumption is plausible because oil prices are dictated by the world market and therefore are unlikely to be affected by movements in Iranian economic and political variables.

Input-Output Models

I-O models quantify the level of connectedness between sectors or firms in a national or regional economy. More specifically, they capture the degree to which the goods and services produced by one sector or firm serve as inputs to the production processes of other sectors or firms. I-O models possess attractive features for analyzing the effects of economic shocks on DIBs. We focus on the abilities to (1) project the effects of a given disruption and (2) provide insight into which types of disruptions may be most costly.

Measuring How a Given Sanctions Package Would Disrupt Each Economic Sector

In terms of projecting the effects of a given disruption, I-O models allow one to identify which industries suffer the most severe reduction in demand as a result of a given disruption. For example, it may be case that a disruption to dominant firms in a given sector is likely to substantially affect other sectors as well. These other sectors may play an integral role in the production of key systems. I-O models can analyze this by tracing how a change in the output of a given entity (such as an industry or firm) affects other entities through backward supply chain linkages, ultimately allowing researchers to project the more-aggregate effects—measured in terms of the reduction in output (the production of final and intermediate goods)—of a relatively isolated initial disruption. This is a desirable capability given that the overall

---

[4] In particular, we examine health spending, social affairs spending, education spending, and economic affairs spending.

magnitude of the reduction in trade is often directly related to key objectives (e.g., the likelihood of the target nation entering into negotiations or the change operational timelines).

Identifying the Most Damaging Sector-Level Disruptions for the Overall Economy and for Targeted Sectors

In terms of providing insights into which types of disruptions may be most costly, I-O models identify the centrality, or criticality, of each sector to national economic production. Centrality is typically considered in a backward sense—how much additional economic activity is required from the suppliers of inputs to a given sector if there is a unit increase in demand for that sector's output. This set of coefficients is referred to as *direct and indirect backward linkages (DIBL) coefficients*. Alternatively, by utilizing a different set of modeling assumptions, one can produce I-O model coefficients that capture centrality in a forward sense—how much economic activity is generated via the sectors that use one unit of a given sector's output as a production input. These are referred to as *direct and indirect forward linkages (DIFL) coefficients*.

There is a second way I-O models can provide insight into the consequences of disruptions that we did not conduct for this analysis, but that merits mention. I-O models can identify how the production of specific goods and services might be disrupted by a shock to a different industry. In contrast with the criticality analysis described in the last paragraph, this analysis looks at damage to a particular sector, rather than at the aggregated amount of damage across all sectors caused by a particular shock. For example, in the context of evaluating the effect of sanctions against Iran, analysis can inform the extent to which Iran's weapons platforms or nuclear capabilities might be affected by a sector-specific package of economic sanctions. It can be challenging to tease out these effects, as supply chains can be complex and extensive. I-O models, through their ability to trace out suppliers of key sectors or firms, allow for data-driven insight into where production may suffer disruption due to a shock.

The DIBL and DIFL coefficients described above capture centrality at the margin: how a relatively small reduction in activity in one sector would affect others. A third type of I-O coefficient, referred to in the results section below as the *sectoral shutdown coefficient*, can speak to broader notions of production centrality: given the sectoral composition of the overall economy, which sectors would most severely depress total output if they were completely shut down—that is, if all economic activity in that sector stopped. An exercise like this incorporates an additional, important dimension: the volume of economic activity that occurs in each sector. In contrast to estimating the production disruption caused by a predetermined disruption, this strand of modeling seeks to instead determine where disruptions would be most harmful.

International Trade Analysis

The last segment of the analysis addresses the international dimension. This component is motivated by the observation that the optimal sanctions package will not solely be determined by the expected effects on the target nation but by how those effects balance against the possible effects on allies, partners, adversaries, and other nations. This trade analysis is focused on how other nations might be affected because they sell to or buy from Iran, and sanctions might disrupt those trade flows. In lieu of conducting a resource-intensive CGE-based analysis, in order to gain a cursory sense of how sanctioning various sectors might affect international trading partners, we analyzed product-level trade data from the UN Comtrade database and the U.S. Energy Information Administration (EIA).[5] We matched the trade data to the corresponding sectors studied in the I-O analysis by assigning traded products to their respective economic sectors. We used 2011 data in model baselines to align the trade analysis with our I-O modeling. Appendix C contains more details on the matching procedures we employed. The primary outputs of our analysis are information on the top export destinations for traded products in the key sectors of the Iranian economy and the corresponding value of exported products; this provides a high-level overview of who is likely to be affected by various sanctions placed on Iran. Unfortunately, technical issues with the UN Comtrade database during

---

[5]   UN Comtrade Database, homepage, undated; U.S. Energy Information Administration, homepage, undated. We used EIA data on Iranian crude oil exports as published in Anthony H. Cordesman, Bryan Gold, Sam Khazai, and Bradley Bosserman, *U.S. and Iranian Strategic Competition: Sanctions, Energy, Arms Control, and Regime Change*, Washington, D.C.: Center for Strategic and International Studies, 2013.

our study prevented us from extending our analysis—for example, to consider imports. This was a result of operational challenges that prevented users from conducting data queries beyond a predetermined threshold. A CGE model would offer higher-fidelity estimates of the change in international trade—for example, by accounting for how nations might react to sanction-induced trade disruptions and how that behavior balances out in equilibrium.

Results

Vector Autoregression

We begin by discussing the results of the VAR analyses. Appendix C provides more-concrete details regarding the structure of each specification and their numerical outputs; here, we focus on the higher-level findings. Our main results can be summarized as follows:

1. A negative shock to oil rents is expected to lead to a significant decline in real GDP over the short term that dissipates over the medium term. This finding supports the literature that argues that the effects of sanctions occur primarily over the first few years, before the target nation has time to adequately adapt to the sanctioning regime.[6] In contrast with the below I-O model results, the VAR model lets us see how the effects are expected to play out over time.

2. We found a significant, persistent decline in military spending following a shock to oil rents. Notably, the estimated effect is larger in magnitude for defense spending than for other forms of government spending; government spending in aggregate is forecasted to initially rise before experiencing a significant and persistent decline. This indicates that sanctions do appear effective at curtailing military spending.

---

[6] Sajjad Faraji Dizaji and Peter A. G. Van Bergeijk, "Potential Early Phase Success and Ultimate Failure of Economic Sanctions: A VAR Approach with an Application to Iran," *Journal of Peace Research*, Vol. 50, No. 6, 2013.

3. The sanctions do not significantly affect the polity score variable over the five-year time horizon we considered. In fact, there is a fairly precisely estimated null effect. This indicates that sanctions do not appear to have an effect on the level of democracy in Iran during the five years following sanctions on oil.

Input-Output Models

Our I-O analysis focused primarily on demonstrating the ability of the approach to identify critical sectors and forecast the effects of sectoral disruptions. Table 5.2 presents separate critical sector rankings according to the three different measures of criticality discussed in the previous section—sectoral shutdown, DIBL, and DIFL—as well as a fourth measure: the weighted average of the DIBL and DIFL coefficients. The table presents distinct lists for the top ten sectors according to each metric. If a U.S. policymaker is most interested in identifying the sectors that will have the greatest overall economic impact if sanctioned, they might focus on the sectoral shutdown coefficient, which suggests that sanctions on four sectors—coke and oil refining, other buildings, energy extraction, and food production—would yield the greatest consequences. More information is contained in Appendix C, such as the magnitudes associated with each sector.

The primary takeaways are the following:

1. The I-O exercises validate many of the sectors that the United States has decided to place sanctions on from an economic perspective. For example, the United States has sanctioned the oil, energy, mining, construction, manufacturing, and shipping sectors, and these same sectors rank highly in economic importance, according to our metrics.
2. The analysis highlights other sectors that would have significant economic consequences if targeted in future rounds of sanctions. These sectors include agriculture, chemical production, and vehicle and equipment production.
3. The sectoral shutdown results demonstrate that model predictions are in the same ballpark as the observed effects of recent sanctions. Between 2018 and 2019, crude oil production in Iran decreased by

TABLE 5.2

Critical Sector Rankings from DIBL, DIFL, and Sectoral Shutdown Input-Output Coefficients

Rank	Sectoral Shutdown	DIBL	DIFL	Weighted Average of DIBL and DIFL
1	Coke- and oil-refining products production	Oil and fats production	Basic aluminum products	Basic aluminum products
2	Other buildings	Production of motor vehicles and other transport equipment, parts, and accessories	Extraction of ferrous metal ores	Aviculture
3	Extraction of crude oil and natural gas	Production, transmission, and distribution of electricity	Coal and lignite mining	Basic iron and steel products
4	Food production	Basic aluminum products	Basic iron and steel products	Oil and fats production
5	Wholesale and retail, except motor vehicles and motorcycles	Aviculture	Mining support services	Production, transmission, and distribution of electricity
6	Residential buildings	Production, repair, and installation of electrical equipment	Production of wood and wooden products, cork, straw, and mat weaving	Other base metals and metal casting
7	Production of motor vehicles and other transport equipment, parts, and accessories	Basic iron and steel products	Aviculture	Mining support services
8	Services of private residential units	Pharmaceutical products, chemicals used in pharmacy and herbal medicinal product production	Warehousing and transportation support activities	Rubber and plastics production

Table 5.2—Continued

Rank	Sectoral Shutdown	DIBL	DIFL	Weighted Average of DIBL and DIFL
9	Chemical materials and products production	Production, repair, and installation of fabricated metal products, excluding machinery and equipment	Pipeline transportation	Production of motor vehicles and other transport equipment, parts, and accessories
10	Defense affairs	Other base metals and metal casting	Recruitment activities	Paper, paper products, and printing production

NOTES: Further information on how each coefficient was calculated, along with their numerical estimates, is contained in Appendix C. Each column contains a list of the top ten most impactful sectors according to the corresponding metric. The Sectoral Shutdown column, for example, is constructed by first estimating the impact on total output of reducing final demand for a sector's output to zero separately for each sector. The list contained in this column then reports the ten sectors that are projected to yield the greatest impact on total output if they experience a shutdown, in order. The other lists are constructed similarly. First, the metric is calculated separately for each sector; then, the table reports the top ten sectors according to projected impact.

41.07 percent, leading GDP to decrease by 6.78 percent. In Appendix C, we demonstrate that the I-O model (based on 2011 data) predicts that a 41.07 percent shock to the crude oil and natural gas sector would reduce total economic output by 3.80 percent.

An important note in evaluating these takeaways is that they speak only to the overall economic consequences of sanctions, under the assumption that more economic damage translates into a higher probability of achieving U.S. objectives. As we will discuss in more detail in the final section of this chapter, this is an oversimplification; more analysis is needed to understand the relationship between overall economic damage from sanctions on Iran and Iran's investment in nuclear weapons capability.

In light of this limiting assumption, it is important to note that this same type of I-O analysis could be applied to determine which sectors most heavily affect output in a given sector, as opposed to which sectors most heavily affect total output. This would be of interest if the goal was to disrupt the production of particular goods and services, such as a weapon platform, as opposed to purely exerting economic pressure. The United States, for example, has sanctioned entities that contribute to weapon production and has restricted dual-use exports in its push to curb nuclear proliferation.[7] Analysis of this sort is not conducted here, though it would follow the same approach.

International Trade Analysis

Lastly, we discuss the observations from our examination of trade flows. For five of the critical sectors listed in the Sectoral Shutdown column of Table 5.2, we report Iran's top ten trading partners in terms of 2011 exports; we focus on sectors in which traded goods account for a substantial amount of economic activity. The top trading partners are shown in Table 5.3. Appendix C contains more-detailed numerical data and additionally reports findings that use two other strategies for matching product-level trade data to our economic sectors of interest.

Table 5.3 highlights the role played by international actors in weighing the pros and cons of different sanctions packages. In 2018, the United States decided to grant six-month waivers to China, India, Japan, South Korea, Taiwan, Turkey, Italy, and Greece after it reimposed a number of sanctions on Iran in order to provide these nations with time to secure alternative sources of oil.[8] It is worth noting that most of these nations are U.S. military allies. In the absence of a waiver, sanctions against Iran could have had the unintended consequence of sending spillover effects into several partner-nation economies. The type of information reported below was used to assist in identifying the waivers. Thus, even simple trade flow analysis can be useful in providing a more-holistic picture of the possible ramifications of economic shocks.

A Notional Framework for Sanctions Policymaking

This case study provides a concrete setting in which we demonstrate ways that the methods we have described could be used to analyze economic

---

[7] Council on Foreign Relations, "International Sanctions on Iran," undated.

[8] "Iran Oil: U.S. to End Sanctions Exemptions for Major Importers," BBC News, April 22, 2019.

TABLE 5.3

Top Export Destinations by Product Sector

Ranking	Extraction of Crude Oil and Natural Gas	Coke- and Oil-Refining Products Production	Food Production	Chemical Materials and Products Production	Production of Motor Vehicles and Other Transport Equipment
1	China	United Arab Emirates	Iraq	China	Iraq
2	Japan	Singapore	Afghanistan	India	United Arab Emirates
3	India	Indonesia	Turkey	United Arab Emirates	Venezuela
4	South Korea	South Korea	Germany	Turkey	Russia
5	Turkey	China	Tajikistan	Afghanistan	Syria
6	Italy	India	Turkmenistan	Belgium	Afghanistan
7	Spain	Japan	Pakistan	Pakistan	Turkmenistan
8	Greece	Ukraine	Azerbaijan	Netherlands	Italy
9	South Africa	Iraq	Vietnam	Iraq	Saudi Arabia
10	France	Turkey	Syria	Indonesia	France

NOTES: The rankings for the extraction of crude oil and natural gas sector are based on crude oil data from the EIA due to the lack of data on export destinations for this sector in the UN Comtrade database. For all other sectors, the rankings displayed in this table result from matching six-digit Harmonized System (HS) product codes to their corresponding International Standard Industrial Classification (ISIC) Revision 4 industries. To accommodate data export restrictions temporarily put in place in the UN Comtrade database, we aggregated the six-digit codes to the four-digit level. This resulted in a number of four-digit product codes mapping to multiple sectors, some of which were outside the scope of our analysis. We chose to include only four-digit product codes for which at least 90 percent of their six-digit extensions corresponded to the target industry. Further details are contained in Appendix C, which also contains results for less-restrictive thresholds.

shocks. VAR models provide value through their ability to project how disruptions are likely to play out over time and through their ability to estimate the effects of a shock on a broad class of key variables. I-O models complement the insight provided by VARs through their ability to quantify production relationships and estimate how a shock may ripple through the broader industrial base and economy. International trade analysis indicates how shocks affecting one nation may affect important U.S. allies, partners, adversaries, and others.

However, such empirical insights alone do not fully exploit the potential of data analysis to support U.S. decisionmakers responsible for managing the consequences (and, more specifically in this case, the occurrence) of economic shocks. For this case study, we argue that a framework could improve the value of empirical analysis by directly tying the analysis to questions such as the following: Will the decline in Iranian defense spending translate into delayed achievement of nuclear weapons capability? Do sanctions cause unacceptable collateral damage in the Iranian economy or to Iran's trade partners? Could an alternative sanctions design avoid or mitigate collateral damage? Is there sufficient confidence in the accuracy of analytic results to rely on them in making decisions?

Assumptions Underlying the Notional Framework

The goal of the remainder of this section is to provide a concrete—if notional—illustration of how a framework might close some of the gaps identified in Chapter Three, as they apply to the Iran sanctions case study. In real-world application, the design of a framework analyzing potential sanctions packages would depend on contextual details that are unknown to us. For expedience, we made assumptions about certain essential details. We assumed that the primary objective of a sanctions package was to delay Iran's acquisition of nuclear weapons, and we assumed that it was undesirable for sanctions to impose substantial collateral damage on the Iranian economy and Iran's trading partners.[9] Moreover, as discussed above, we assumed that the two potential ways in which decisionmakers envision that sanctions might work were by generating domestic political pressure on the government to stop nuclear research in order to end sanctions and by imposing fiscal pressure that reduced funds available for nuclear weapons R&D.

---

[9] We also assumed that "substantial" could be quantified, although we did not need to specify this quantification in this narrative.

Framework Architecture

We envision a framework for this scenario as embedding several distinct modules, which are summarized in Figure 5.1. One module might focus on estimating the effectiveness of sanctions packages in achieving U.S. objectives. This module might account for both potential mechanisms of effectiveness: political pressure and budgetary pressure. A second module might assess the direct and indirect costs of imposing each sanctions package. Direct costs might include the administrative costs of imposing and enforcing sanctions. Indirect costs might include estimation of collateral damage. Finally, we envision a module that would facilitate comparison of COAs by examining the trade-off between effectiveness and cost for each alternative. Any of these three modules—effectiveness, costs, and trade-offs of COAs—might have multiple levels of submodules below them.

Sanctions Effectiveness Module and Submodules

A primary objective of the effectiveness module might be to identify the circumstances under which sanctions would achieve U.S. objectives. Some examined circumstances might have implications for module design and

FIGURE 5.1
Architecture of the Notional Iran Sanctions Framework

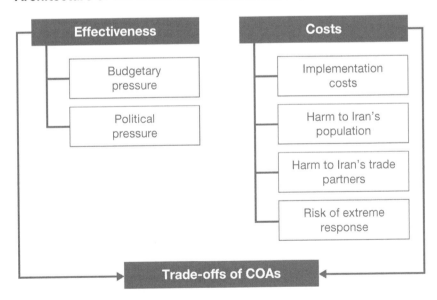

execution—for example, identifying which sectors to sanction, how severely to sanction them, for what duration, and at what time. The module for sanctions effectiveness might incorporate distinct submodules for the two mechanisms—political and budgetary pressure. These modules might project the Iran government's budget choices in response to the budgetary and political pressures imposed by the sanctions. The budgetary pressure submodule might consider factors such as the government's latitude to cut budgetary components, the economic consequences of cutting various budgetary components, and the government's ability to increase revenue through nonsanctioned economic transactions. The political pressure submodule might consider the economic consequences of sanctions for key political constituencies, political and economic consequences of cutting various budgetary components, and even analyses of the personalities and motives of those in key leadership positions. Perhaps the most difficult part of the entire framework might be the design of a well-calibrated model of the governance mechanism whereby economic damage from the sanctions translates into political pressure sufficient to change the Iranian government's pursuit of nuclear weapons capability.

Sanctions Costs Module and Submodules

The United States might incur direct and indirect costs as a result of imposing sanctions on Iran, and the magnitude of these costs might vary across different sanctions packages. Direct costs might include the cost of implementing and enforcing sanctions. Indirect costs might include unintentional consequences of the sanctions, such as economic damage to Iran's trading partners or suffering by the Iranian population. Furthermore, severe economic and political effects of sanctions might carry the risk of extreme responses contrary to U.S. interests, such as regional instability. The costs module might incorporate multiple submodules to examine the likelihood and severity of each of these potential costs under various sanctions COAs.

Module for Comparing Trade-Offs Across Potential Sanctions Courses of Action

The third notional module would synthesize the results of the effectiveness and costs modules, with the objective of helping decisionmakers evaluate the trade-offs of each COA. This module might be central to the design and interpretation of empirical analysis, since this module might identify the decision boundaries between COAs, specifying what empirical results would favor one COA versus another.

This module might identify a *trade-off acceptability boundary* that specifies ranges of acceptable and unacceptable trade-offs between sanctions effectiveness and sanctions costs. Then empirical analysis could focus on estimating on which side of that boundary each potential sanctions package is located. Similarly, this module could help determine whether available data could be used to estimate the location of each sanctions package relative to the boundary with sufficient precision to satisfy decisionmaker requirements for confidence in estimates.

Framework Output

We envision that the final output of the framework would be a mapping of analytic findings to sanctions decisions, which would then be used to design empirical analyses and interpret findings. In reality, the process of designing the framework, designing the empirical analysis, and executing the empirical analysis might not proceed linearly; there might be substantial iteration between these three steps to help calibrate the framework and refine options.[10]

---

[10] The research team does not know how these decisions are currently made and what analytic support exists. This exercise is purely notional and is intended to convey the concept of a framework in a concrete setting. Undoubtedly, it misses many key elements that actual analysis and decisionmaking would need to incorporate.

CHAPTER SIX

Conclusions and Recommendations

Economic shocks are unanticipated changes in the conditions upon which resource allocation decisions are based. The main pathway by which this report envisions an economic shock degrading military capability is by changing allocation decisions of entities in a DIB or its supply chain, leading to disruptions such as cost increases or supply limitations. The concern underlying this study is the possibility that economic shocks could induce the same effects as classic kinetic supply interdiction efforts: the destruction of war materiel, the diversion of resources from high-priority military initiatives, and the imposition of costs. A key assertion underlying this study is that the United States, its allies, and its adversaries might be differentially exposed to the deleterious consequences of some economic shocks because each country has a distinct economic structure. Consequently, under certain conditions, an economic shock might impart an asymmetric military advantage by more severely affecting some countries' DIBs and economies.

We propose that three sets of features drive the effects of economic shocks on military capability: features of the shock event itself, features of the DIB under consideration, and features related to the response and adaptation of affected entities. From this perspective, managing the effects of economic shocks on the generation of DIB capability is facilitated by an understanding of the sensitivity of outcomes to these features and the development of tools for influencing key malleable features.

Yet several technical challenges pose obstacles to leveraging available data to measure system sensitivity. We identified four such challenges:

1. It can be difficult to identify the mathematical structure of the relationship between shock outcomes and features.

2. It can be difficult to distinguish between meaningful measurements and statistical noise, or random variation.

3. The relationships between shock outcomes and features can change over time, especially as decisionmakers in economies, markets, and supply chains adapt over time to earlier shocks.

4. It can be difficult to assess whether relationships are measured with sufficient accuracy to support decisionmaking.

In light of the centrality of DIB capability in an era of near-peer competition, DARPA asked RAND NSRD to explore the potential value of existing methods from economics in overcoming the technical challenges to data-informed management of the defense implications of economic shocks. An expansive economics literature on shocks has grappled with similar issues. But since the resulting methods were developed for different purposes, the extent to which they satisfy the analytic requirements of the envisioned defense applications is unclear. RAND's research team framed the analysis by focusing on several core questions:

- What are the questions of interest that defense decisionmakers need addressed to manage the effects of economic shocks on DIBs?
- What are today's workhorse methods for modeling the effects of these shocks?
- What are the challenges to addressing the questions of interest with existing methods and approaches?
- What would a new approach look like, and how could a new DARPA program help to improve capability?

To approach these questions, we employed multiple research lines of effort, which are described in Chapters Two through Five of this report. Following the introduction to the problem in Chapter One, in Chapter Two we explored several vignettes to identify core management concerns that decisionmakers might face and important contextual features that an analytic capability should be able to incorporate—what we term *analytic capability requirements*. In Chapter Three, we discussed the four key technical challenges to operationalizing the envisioned analytic capability. We also analyzed the gap between existing methodological capabilities and what is required to meet the analytic capability requirements suggested by the vignettes. We found that economics uses several methodologies to assess systemic shocks and their sectoral or systemic effects, of which four are highlighted. All have both strengths and demonstrable weaknesses. What they share is an inability in themselves to be solely sufficient for defense officials to anticipate, detect, understand potential consequences from, or frame policies to hedge against or manage the results of such shocks.

An important gap to achieving the analytic capability requirements is that existing empirical methods cannot always overcome the technical challenges to achieving the analytic capability requirements. The validity of any empirical method depends on data that are not always available and on assumptions that may not always be reasonable in real-world application. Moreover, while not technically a gap, we explored an additional drawback of existing empirical methods. In applying existing methods, the selection, construction, and calibration of empirical analysis would depend on the context of the applied environment, precluding plug-and-play analysis; analyses must be tailored to each application.

This finding might seem to suggest that better empirical methods are needed to overcome the challenges and limitations. However, there are at least two reasons to think that investments in better-performing empirical methods might not be the low-hanging fruit for improving analytic support to defense decisionmakers. First, enormous effort has been put in across empirical economics and econometrics literature to overcoming the core technical challenges discussed above: achieving inference with a quantifiable and sufficient level of confidence in poor data environments and with limited understanding of the underlying mechanisms driving effects. It is possible that the investment required to significantly improve performance might exceed the benefits of that improved performance. Second, there is a gap aside from empirical methodology that would limit the value of even the best possible empirical analysis and that might be more cost-effectively addressed.

The second significant gap we found is that even where existing methods are able to overcome the technical challenges, the data analysis alone is insufficient to inform decisionmaker choices. Additional analysis may be needed to provide context to the data analysis in a way that can inform decisionmaking. More specifically, additional analysis is often needed to determine which empirical analyses should be conducted and to translate empirical results into implications for the COAs under consideration. The additional analysis required typically is multidisciplinary and may entail both quantitative and qualitative methods.

In Chapter Four, we introduced the construct of frameworks tailored to each applied environment that we propose would help close the gaps identified in Chapter Three. The frameworks capture the decision-relevant mechanisms affecting shock instigation, propagation, and effects. One way to view this function of a framework is as a facilitator of the orientation phase of an OODA loop representing the process of managing the consequences of an economic shock; the main objective of a framework is to connect analytic outputs to COAs under consideration for managing shock consequences. Frameworks can also help overcome the technical challenges to achieving analytic capabilities and can help identify what analyses should be conducted.

In Chapter Four, we also presented a preliminary and partial framework for shock-induced supply restriction. In this framework, for a shock of a given latency, the faster decisionmakers can proceed through OODA loops to effectively respond to a shock and thereby avoid or mitigate damage, the less damage the shock will cause. The supply restriction framework proposes heuristics for identifying shock latency. It then identifies several potential modeling considerations for each latency. Shock latency therefore serves as a mechanism to identify the appropriate analytic approach. Short-latency shocks can potentially affect ongoing combat operations. Long-latency shocks are most relevant in long-term competition, affecting production capabilities and technology. In between these extremes is an intermediate-latency category characterized by shock outcomes that are most sensitive to features of the shock and the applied environment. We propose that intermediate-latency shocks might be the most interesting from the perspective of U.S. defense leaders, since at this latency, the race between shock propagation and the response of shocked nations is potentially most competitive and is therefore where risks and opportunities are greatest.

In Chapter Five, we made the analyses and arguments of Chapters Two and Three more concrete and precise through application to a recent historical instance of an intentionally triggered economic shock: U.S. sanctions on Iran. Here in Chapter Six, we synthesize the key findings from our analysis into two recommendations based on those findings.

Recommendations to the Department of Defense for Advancing Models for Measuring the Effects of Economic Shocks on Defense Postures

Recommendation 1: Invest in a Research Program

The synthesis of Findings 1 through 3 led us to our first recommendation. Evidence from the vignettes suggests our first finding: that economic shocks could pose severe risks to defense capability. Our second finding is that a modest portfolio of analytic capabilities would support data-driven management of the effects of shocks. Our third finding is that four workhorse empirical methods from economics make substantial contributions to providing those analytic capabilities. In combination, these findings suggest that there might be opportunities to achieve cost-effective advancements in providing analytic support to defense decisionmakers.

More specifically, evidence suggests that across the portfolio of analytic capability requirements, there are some capability requirements that could be substantially met through straightforward application of existing empirical methods in the manner demonstrated by the Iran sanctions case study. Although precisely estimating the costs and benefits of investments needed to operationalize these capabilities is beyond the scope of this study, given the potential severity of the risks posed by economic shocks and the relatively small gaps to achieving some of the analytic capability requirements, in our judgment, it is likely that relatively small investments have a high likelihood of yielding improvements in shock management worth the cost. On the other hand, the gap to achieving other analytic capability requirements will require substantially more investment, and the value of the resulting toolkit is less certain.

In light of these assessments, we recommend that DARPA or another defense entity invest in a program to advance data-informed management of economic shocks.[1] As discussed below, such a program should include experts from an array of disciplines, potentially including economics, political science, organizational behavior, sociology, and military studies (strategy and planning). The program performance base should include economists proficient in the application of workhorse models from economics, but additional disciplinary representation is needed to ensure that analysis informs decisions that are pertinent for defense decisionmakers.

Given uncertainty over the relative costs and benefits of overall program investment and the apparent heterogeneity in cost-benefit ratio across different potential program investments, the performers could start by addressing analytic capability requirements with the broadest applicability or lowest investment cost—the low-hanging fruit—to both achieve early operational gains and build a base of knowledge that will be helpful for addressing more-challenging capability requirements. For instance, early program objectives could include embedding the workhorse empirical methods from economics into existing applications across DoD that would benefit from the economic insights they provide. In doing so, performers will build a base of knowledge about fundamental empirical challenges, such as identifying and measuring shocks and their consequences under a range of data environments, which will provide a base of knowledge lowering the marginal investment needed to develop more technically challenging and risky capability requirements.

Recommendation 2: Root Program Design and Implementation in Scenarios and Their Associated Management Choices

Our second recommendation stems from our fourth and fifth findings. Our fourth finding is that the workhorse empirical methods cannot always overcome the technical challenges to achieving the analytic capability requirements. The fifth finding is that additional analysis beyond the type of system parameter estimation provided by the workhorse empirical methods

---

[1] As a federally funded research and development center, the RAND National Defense Research Institute is not eligible to serve as a performer on contracts conducting research for such a program.

is needed to fully exploit the potential of data analysis to support defense decisionmakers. The synthesis of these findings leads to our second recommendation, that execution of a program in advancing data-informed management of economic shocks be grounded in specific policy questions and management decisions.

Grounding program execution in specific analytic decisions can support successful program outcomes by reducing the multiplicity of potential empirical designs. The range of appropriate empirical approaches should be narrowed based on central features, such as data environment, the time horizon over which analytic insights are needed, and relevant shock mechanisms. One especially potent simplifying approach is to start by establishing how analytic outcomes help distinguish between alternative management choices. This tethering enables empirical analysis to focus on illuminating the boundary between alternative decisions rather than the entire potential space of outcomes. Put differently, ensuring adequate precision of analytic findings is a daunting technical challenge, especially in data-poor environments; focusing analytic efforts on where variation in analytic outcomes supports alternative decisions potentially reduces the performance requirement on empirical approaches, increasing chances of success.

A way to implement this recommendation is to focus each program increment on a set of historical and hypothetical scenarios in which each scenario is defined by a specific decision and context, but each scenario in the increment shares a common dimension relevant to that increment's objective. For instance, one program increment might have program performers develop analytic support for several different scenarios focused on long-term competition supply restrictions. Scenarios might differ by the countries, industries, or policy levers on which they focus but might all be oriented toward a common challenge associated with that type of scenario.

Drawing on both historical and hypothetical scenarios might enable synergies, since historical scenarios enable some amount of validation against actual outcomes, while hypothetical scenarios encourage less-bounded consideration of how shock-related concerns might manifest in modern technological, economic, and geopolitical environments.

Concluding Remarks

The 2018 National Defense Strategy characterizes the global security environment as having reentered an era of peer and near-peer competition. In such a security domain, industrial capability is emerging as a decisive margin of military advantage. A nation's ability to marshal industrial resources to quickly field sophisticated and reliable weapon systems forms the foundation of power projection in support of national objectives. The sophistication of modern weapon systems increasingly defies reactive defenses and countermeasures. In this regard, system features such as lethality, survivability, stealth, physical speed, and information-processing rates all contribute to their overall capability.

Even as weapon systems' technological sophistication has challenged traditional defenses, the globalization of trade and finance has inexorably exposed weapon system supply chains to turbulent economic forces, or shocks. With their growth in sophistication, these weapon systems may rely on elements provided by a variety of sectors, including microelectronics, specialized metals and composites, and energy resources. Shocks to critical supply chains can yield disruption in the production and readiness of those weapon systems. But production also draws on other key economic inputs, such as access to appropriate capital (both physical and financial), labor, land, and technology resources. As a result, the threat that economic shocks pose to weapon system availability and readiness can be quite broad and consequential. Indeed, the likelihood of shock events might exceed the consideration that such shocks receive in current acquisitions processes, logistics planning and operations, and military doctrine.

DARPA and other defense stakeholders have initiated efforts to enhance the ability of the U.S. government to manage the risks that economic shocks pose to the generation of defense capabilities. In this report, we have examined the potential of existing empirical methods from economics to inform decisionmaking related to such management. We find that there is significant untapped potential for these methods to support decisionmakers but that more work is needed to operationalize data-driven approaches. Given the potential for significant damage that the economic shocks appear to pose for DIB capability and the promising capabilities of existing methods, we propose that DARPA or another defense entity invest in a program to harness these capabilities. In this report, we propose potential first steps and scenarios that could be used as guideposts for evaluating the progress of the program. We anticipate that there is variation in the amount of effort needed to operationalize enhanced data-driven decisionmaking: There are likely useful capabilities that can be realized through relatively straight-forward extensions of existing institutional and methodological resources. Building other capabilities might require significant investment over time. In our estimation, there is good reason to be concerned about the risk that economic shocks pose to defense capabilities. It is our hope that the research presented in this report provides useful insight on how to proceed in capably managing these risks.

Literature Review of Economic Shocks

The purpose of this appendix is to describe the literature review we conducted in order to home in on the four workhorse empirical methods used in economics for studying shocks. The economics literature on shocks is extensive and diverse: Economists have examined many different types of shocks under many different conditions and have been concerned with a diverse array of outcomes. Ex ante, one would not necessarily expect just a few methods to be useful across such a wide range of studies. In fact, studies have used a wide variety of methods, but many of those methods are used in a small minority of papers. It turns out that just four methods (and variations thereof) are used in a significant majority of the papers that we reviewed.

This appendix proceeds as follows. First, we provide a high-level overview of the empirical economics literature on shocks: how shocks are defined and the two fundamental tasks that empirical methods seek to achieve—identifying shocks and predicting the effects of shocks. Second, we describe the four methods that appear most frequently in the literature we reviewed. Finally, we describe our process for selecting the literature we reviewed and describe selected important and representative papers in that selection, many of which use the four workhorse methods we describe in the second section of this appendix.

This presentation of material does not reflect the sequence of our literature review. In execution, we first narrowed the scope of our literature review to shocks that are especially salient to the defense questions under consideration in this project (trade, agricultural, oil, labor, and financial shocks), and then we conducted a thorough review of published papers focused on these types of shocks. During this literature review, we noted the striking similarity of methods used across these (still-extensive) bodies of literature. In this appendix, we describe the methods that came out of our literature review before we describe the literature review itself, as it might be hard to understand without prior understanding of the models.

Overview of How Economists Have Defined and Studied Shocks

The economics literature includes a significant body of work concerned with estimating the effects of economic shocks on various outcomes of interest. What exactly is an *economic shock*? In addition to describing other shock characteristics, Ramey argues that shocks "should represent either unanticipated movements in exogenous variables or news about future movements in exogenous variables."[1] By *exogenous variables*, we mean variables whose value is determined outside of a given model; as such, which variables qualify as exogenous will be model dependent. A shock, then, can be thought of as an unforeseen event that either positively or negatively affects such endogenous economic variables as employment, prices, or output.

The relationship between an event and its consequences can be estimated in either a predictive or causal fashion. Predictive models aim to forecast, or project into the future, the effects of shocks by answering questions such as "When I observe that X increases by some amount, by how much do I expect Y to increase?" The change in Y may occur as a direct result of the change in X or through other variables that are correlated with X. In contrast, causal models ask, "What part of the observed change in Y is caused by an increase in X?" Such models aim to isolate the contribution of X to movements in Y. Researchers can estimate the relationship between sets of variables using theoretical models, empirical models, or some combination of the two. In a theoretical framework, this is done by "shocking" an exogenous variable and examining how doing so affects endogenous variables.

---

[1]   Valerie A Ramey, "Macroeconomic Shocks and Their Propagation," Chapter 2 in John B. Taylor and Herald Uhlig, eds., *Handbook of Macroeconomics*, Vol. 2, Amsterdam: Elsevier, 2016.

Empirically, statistical models are developed to understand how variation in one variable (or set of variables) relates to variation in others. This section provides an overview of a set of modeling approaches that can be used to analyze various aspects of the DIB and the supply chains it is composed of. It covers both techniques for statistically detecting shocks and methods for projecting their effects.

There are various ways that shocks can be identified. Narrative methods involve examining historical records to track down the reason for and magnitude of a change in a given variable. Hamilton, 1985, used this approach to identify political events that drove changes in oil markets.[2] It is also common to impose restrictions on regression coefficients or parameters in order to identify shocks. Restrictions can involve the timing of effects, the direction (sign) of effects (positive or negative), or outside estimates based on empirical evidence or economic theory. Brinca, Duarte, and Faria-e-Castro, 2020, used sign restrictions coupled with outside estimates to measure labor supply and demand shocks by sector and month during part of the COVID-19 pandemic.[3] Another strategy is to employ an *instrumental variable* to estimate the causal effect of a shock. An instrument is used when the explanatory variable of interest is correlated with the error term in a regression, which could occur for any number of reasons. An instrumental variable affects the dependent variable only through its relation to the explanatory variable of interest, thereby allowing the researcher to estimate the causal effect of the explanatory variable on the dependent variable. Berton et al., 2018, used an instrumental variable approach to isolate the exogenous component of credit supply to study the effects of a credit supply shock on firm employment.[4] One can also estimate a fully specified and calibrated theoretical model to back out an implied series of shocks. Smets and Wouters, 2007, used this method to produce estimates of technology,

---

[2] James D. Hamilton, "Historical Causes of Postwar Oil Shocks and Recessions," *The Energy Journal*, Vol. 6, No. 1, 1985.

[3] Pedro Brinca, Joao B. Duarte, and Miguel Faria-e-Castro, "Measuring Labor Supply and Demand Shocks During COVID-19," St. Louis, Mo.: Federal Reserve Bank of St. Louis, Working Paper 2020-011D, 2020.

[4] Fabio Berton, Sauro Mocetti, Andrea F. Presbitero, and Matteo Richiardi, "Banks, Firms, and Jobs," *Review of Financial Studies*, Vol. 31, No. 6, 2018.

risk premium, and other shocks.[5] The above discussion does not represent an exhaustive list of shock identification methodologies but rather provides examples of commonly used approaches that are salient to DIB research.

Workhorse Methodologies for Estimating the Effects of Shocks

Identifying shocks is typically only part of what the existing research attempts to accomplish. Frequently, research also attempts to understand the effects of shocks. In fact, identifying shocks and measuring their consequences often go hand in hand. This is because it is difficult to discuss estimating shocks in a vacuum, since the exogeneity condition is typically a function of the estimating equation (i.e., it is model dependent). Consequently, there is a wide range of possible ways to measure the effects of shocks.

Our literature review, described in the next section, found that four types of methods are workhorse methods, used most frequently across the papers we reviewed: (1) VARs, (2) I-O models, (3) CGE models, and (4) PR models. Papers using other types of methods often have distinctive research questions or circumstances. Between the four workhorse models, researchers can estimate firm-level effects, such as those on employment, prices, wages, stock prices, production, credit availability and quality, investment, and default; sector-level outcomes, such as labor productivity, capital stock, revenue, imports, exports, and industrial production; and national-level outcomes, such as GDP growth, consumption, price changes, and interest rate movements—just to name a few. Moreover, they can capture spillover effects on different entities and estimate effects at different frequencies. Some models produce before-and-after style estimates; some produce short-term, dynamic forecasts; and others produce long-term, dynamic forecasts. As is discussed in Chapter Three, the choice of which model to use will depend on what question is being asked and what data are available.

---

5   Frank Smets and Rafael Wouters, "Shocks and Frictions in U.S. Business Cycles: A Bayesian DSGE Approach," *American Economic Review*, Vol. 97, No. 3, 2007.

VARs were used in all four shock types that we analyzed. VARs are stochastic process models that capture interdependencies among a set of time series data and recursively generate forecasts. In a VAR, each variable is a function of lagged values of all other variables and an error term, resulting in recursive forecast generation. The same model can be used both to identify shocks and to examine their effects. Furthermore, the model is also flexible with respect to time, so the range of possible time frames (daily, quarterly, or annual) allows for application to several types of data and shock. Additionally, VARs are shown to have good forecasting performance.[6] However, VARs also have some limitations. The flexibility in usage is paired with a lack of theoretical basis for choosing variables and structural relationship details. Identification assumptions can be guided by theory. The recursive nature of a VAR estimate also leads to the compounding of forecast error if the model is misspecified.

I-O modeling was used in trade, oil, and financial shock analysis. I-O models quantify the connectedness among sectors or firms in a national or regional economy and are often used to project how a shock to a given sector or firm propagates through other sectors or firms to the broader economy. The level of detail in an I-O model can vary greatly depending on the need. For example, the most granular I-O modeling allows for firm-level analysis. Furthermore, the parameters regarding linkages between firms in this context can explicitly capture network and supply chain effects, both within and across industries. However, I-O model specification tends to be static and linear; thus, the models do not consider behavioral aspects of responses. Furthermore, the assumptions and parameters regarding interfirm or interindustry relationships may not be plausible in the long run as technological shifts occur. In such cases, dynamic estimations require heavy assumptions.

CGE modeling is used extensively in the trade and agricultural models that we describe here. It is also used in some oil shock models. CGE models are simulation-based optimization models that generate shock effect estimates through modeling how households, firms, and the government optimize their behavior given the constraints they face. Because it is generalizable, CGE modeling captures both optimizing and reactive behavior among

---

[6] James H. Stock and Mark W. Watson, "Vector Autoregressions," *Journal of Economic Perspectives*, Vol. 15, No. 4, 2001.

agents in the DIB and other parts of the economy (households, firms, and government). Furthermore, as a generalized representation of economic activity, the models can simultaneously capture both upstream and downstream effects. However, CGE modeling is very resource intensive. Additionally, because of the equilibrium-forecasting nature of the technique, the identification assumptions that allow for a solvable equilibrium in the long run may not be plausible in the short run. Further assumptions are required to estimate dynamic quantities. Thus, CGE modeling is best suited for comparison of pre- and post-shock equilibria. Furthermore, key variables salient to the DIB may be captured only at a relatively aggregated level using this technique.

PR methods were used extensively in financial shock models and to some extent in oil shock models. PR models are a broad class of models applied to data on a given set of entities that are tracked over time. They are linked through a shared goal of trying to isolate exogenous variation in an explanatory variable to identify its causal effect on a dependent variable. PR is a flexible technique that can be adapted to many different scenarios. Depending on the underlying model and data availability, PR methods may achieve reduced-form causal analysis through such PR methods as difference in differences, instrumental variable, event study, or fixed effect techniques, to name a few. Furthermore, a well-understood and versatile array of identification assumptions allows for precisely estimated effects. However, this technique is generally static. It is not ideal for long-run analysis and not well suited for dynamic forecasts. In addition, its application across shocks may be idiosyncratic. This increases the restructuring effort needed and decreases the comparability achievable in examining different shocks and scenarios.

Literature Review Details for Selected Shock Types

In this appendix section, we describe our review of the literature for selected types of shocks. Existing research in economics has identified several types of economic shocks; we start with an explanation of how we selected shock types on which to focus.

As discussed in Chapter Two, we organized common shock types according to whether they are market derived, are non-market derived, or result from economic policy. Within this baseline typology, we narrowed the scope of our literature search based on a few representative domains that could be of keen interest to DoD stakeholders. Since we are concerned with peacetime factors that affect the production capabilities of the DIB, our narrowed scope focused on shock types that affect firm-level and industry-level production functions and supply chains. We also used familiarity with macroeconomic literature to pick shock categories that were more common, since we anticipated that these would have a wide range of pursuant methodologies published in the mainstream literature. In the following review, we discuss a study's implications for defense-related production functions and supply chains, although they are often not explicitly mentioned in the analysis.

Pursuant to the filtering and consolidation criteria described above, we decided to focus on trade, agricultural, oil, labor, and financial shocks. After initial review, we concluded that the bulk of the agricultural literature involved trade-related analysis because of the globally substitutable nature of agricultural commodity production and consumption, so we merged the two categories. Trade and agriculture shocks included both manmade and natural (e.g., crop failure) shocks. Oil shocks were generally defined as sudden large movements in the price of oil. Labor shocks were broadly defined to include supply, demand, and policy shocks. Financial shocks were broadly defined to include fiscal policy, monetary policy, and credit conditions resulting from financial events. For many analyses, the shock is defined narratively based on observed abrupt changes in price; in these situations, the economic analysis attempts to isolate the relative contributions of structural demand innovations, structural supply innovations, and policy constraints to the price change. Examples of each type of shock are as follows:

- Agricultural, trade, and commodity shocks could take the form of movements in global commodity markets, changes in agricultural productivity, or changes in tariffs or quotas. Such events could threaten readiness because of regionally restricted access to Class I supply (rations, including food, drinking water, and health and comfort items), for example.

- An oil shock may represent an unanticipated increase or decrease in oil supply or demand. Oil shocks have the potential to disrupt polymer production and availability, as well as access to the supply of operational energy.
- Labor shocks include shifts in (industry-specific) labor supply or demand, which could have numerous impacts. For highly specialized labor, shocks could create potential disruption at the weapon system–specific level. For less-specialized labor, there could be disruption across the DIB in production or distribution. For agglomerated industries, there may be a more targeted disruption within a sector that could affect, for example, Class VIIIa supply (medical consumable supplies, not including blood or blood products).
- Financial shocks include unexpected changes in uncertainty and movements in credit spreads. They may extend the timelines needed for multiyear procurements and execution of block buy contracts, may slow down upkeep and improvements for capital-intensive facilities, and could create ripple effects across the DIB in securing access to financial capital.

As we reviewed the literature for these four types of shock, we sought to capture the relevant research questions, methodologies, and data sources used in academic research. Furthermore, we noted distinctions in shock definitions, as well as estimates of the time to impact and the duration of the effects. In this section, we report analyses of shocks that fit our intermediate-latency categorization. In other words, we include analyses of shocks that could conceivably propagate through the DIB's salient markets and supply chains to cause operational or production disruptions in a time frame beyond a stockpile buffer but shorter than a Future Years Defense Program. We reviewed academic research dating as far back as 1980, but here we report mostly methodologies used in recent papers analyzing shocks. However, to the extent that older analytic techniques are not proven to be demonstrably *wrong*, they are still potentially useful in analyzing economic shocks of the future. This is particularly true if older methods are simpler to execute, are easier for decisionmakers to interpret, or can be easily automated using existing or future technology. Put differently, methodologies considered best practices or state of the art for analyzing shocks tend to have been developed fairly recently, but the age of a methodology itself is not an indication of its value. Some older methods developed as far back as the 1980s might still be considered best.

Trade and Agriculture Shocks

International trade in goods and services is particularly susceptible to sudden changes caused by policy levers. This economic activity is also subject to unpredictable shocks, such as crop failures that are due to natural disasters. Finally, the spread of technology across producers can rapidly change production possibilities. Such developments can quickly alter the global input landscape for firms in the DIB. For example, readiness could be reduced due to regionally restricted access to Class I supply.

Dixon, Rimmer, and Tsigas, 2007, used a CGE model at the subnational (regional) level in analyzing the effects of import policy shocks (e.g., tariffs and quotas) on many economic indicators for U.S. regions, such as capital stock, employment, demand, prices, and import/export volumes.[7] Regional modeling is important since regional economic conditions may disproportionately affect certain DIB production facilities. The CGE approach was extended in a timely modeling analysis after the imposition of U.S. "trade war" tariffs in 2018, as provided by Li, Balistreri, and Zhang, 2020.[8] They used CGE modeling with international trade input variables, such as trade flow volumes and tariff rates. The variables are combined with domestic economic measures such as employment, compensation, expenditures, and commodity demands in the equilibrium modeling. Their partial- and general-equilibrium modeling approach allows for prediction of the medium-term change in key commodity prices that would be experienced in Iowa, an agricultural state heavily exposed to the tariffs. Import policy

[7] Peter B. Dixon, Maureen T. Rimmer, and Marinos E. Tsigas, "Regionalising Results from a Detailed CGE Model: Macro, Industry and State Effects in the U.S. of Removing Major Tariffs and Quotas," *Papers in Regional Science*, Vol. 86, No. 1, 2007.

[8] Minghao Li, Edward J. Balistreri, and Wendong Zhang, "The U.S.–China Trade War: Tariff Data and General Equilibrium Analysis," *Journal of Asian Economics*, Vol. 69, 2020.

changes also constitute one shock type analyzed by Acemoglu, Akcigit, and Kerr, 2016.[9] They used an I-O modeling approach to estimate aggregate economy-wide changes in value added, employment, and labor productivity in response to abrupt changes in tariff policy—specifically, U.S. county-level trade exposure to Chinese import competition. In all these analyses, macroeconomic impacts and their likely attendant political consequences are an important consideration for predicting DIB consequences from trade shocks.

Alam and Gilbert, 2017, explored the impact of monetary policy shocks on agricultural price signals. They utilized SVAR and factor-augmented vector autoregression (FAVAR) techniques, with input variables including global commodity price indexes, U.S. crop storage inventories and crop yields, global macroeconomic conditions, financial conditions, and real interest rates—which are subject to shocks by the Federal Reserve policy-makers.[10] De Winne and Peersman, 2016, similarly used SVAR for modeling the U.S. macroeconomic response to shocks in global food commodity markets.[11] Global food commodity shocks are defined in two ways: by inputting a global production index into the SVAR model and by separately estimating effects in the SVAR of 13 narratively defined global food price shocks. Food is possibly the most important traded commodity, so a thorough understanding of responses to food-related shocks is necessary for understanding the security landscape of any country or region.

Lee, 2018, analyzed weather-induced crop failures in a static CGE model.[12] Rainfall is an input in the model, which also includes common production measures such as establishments, employment, wages and sala-

---

[9] Daron Acemoglu, Ufuk Akcigit, and William Kerr, "Networks and the Macroeconomy: An Empirical Exploration," *NBER Macroeconomics Annual*, Vol. 30, No. 1, 2016.

[10] Md Rafayet Alam and Scott Gilbert, "Monetary Policy Shocks and the Dynamics of Agricultural Commodity Prices: Evidence from Structural and Factor-Augmented VAR Analyses," *Agricultural Economics*, Vol. 48, No. 1, 2017.

[11] Jasmien De Winne and Gert Peersman, "Macroeconomic Effects of Disruptions in Global Food Commodity Markets: Evidence for the United States," *Brookings Papers on Economic Activity 2016*, No. 2, 2016.

[12] Iona Hyojung Lee, "Industrial Output Fluctuations in Developing Countries: General Equilibrium Consequences of Agricultural Productivity Shocks," *European Economic Review*, Vol. 102, 2018.

ries, value added, and gross fixed capital formation. Thus, rainfall and the other variables of the CGE model are used to attempt to explain import and export volumes, as well as agriculture's share of GDP. Climate change–induced multiyear variations in weather patterns across the globe may play a destabilizing force for the better part of the 21st century, so methods for predicting their economic and security outputs are a key security asset for a DIB with global inputs and global capability demands.

Oil Shocks

From the early 20th century through to the beginning of the 21st, oil has been a particularly important input commodity. Its subsequent uses in power generation, transportation, and plastic-making place it high on many supply chains, which then have the potential to become especially susceptible to price swings. Several instances of large price changes have been noted by the general public and studied by economists. These events include the spike around the 1973 OPEC embargo, the crash around the 2020 COVID-19 pandemic lockdowns, and many events in the intervening years. Supply restrictions, demand competition, and the ensuing price volatility have the potential to degrade operational performance of the DIB. For example, impediments to acquiring oil would disrupt polymer production and availability, as well as the energy needed for ongoing operations and transportation.

VAR is used extensively in recent analyses of oil shocks, and I-O, CGE, and PR methods are also present. Kilian, 2008, asked whether exogenous oil supply shocks explain changes in the real price of oil and whether there are dynamic effects on U.S. real GDP growth and Consumer Price Index inflation.[13] This analysis uses PR techniques. Further investigation by Kilian, 2009, used SVAR modeling to identify and estimate the dynamic price effects of demand and supply shocks in the global crude oil market.[14] The SVAR model includes monthly data covering oil production, oil prices,

---

[13] Lutz Kilian, "Exogenous Oil Supply Shocks: How Big Are They and How Much Do They Matter for the U.S. Economy?" *Review of Economics and Statistics*, Vol. 90, No. 2, 2008.

[14] Kilian, 2009.

and global real economic activity. As stated above, the price of oil will continue to be intricately connected to the business environment and financial outlook for almost all firms in the DIB, until we reach a future in which fossil fuels are obsolete. Thus, methods to anticipate swings in the price of oil provide critical business intelligence as the DIB seeks to create needed capabilities.

In a recent methodological innovation, Baumeister and Hamilton, 2019, developed a BSVAR for oil markets.[15] Dependent variables include world production, spot price, and domestic U.S crude stock. They also considered global economic activity by creating an industrial production index for several major exporters: members of OPEC and Brazil, Russia, India, China, and South Africa (BRICS), which are also significant energy producers. In the BSVAR, oil-related input variables were separated into three categories: oil supply shocks, aggregate economy-wide demand shocks, and oil-specific demand shocks. As above, this recently developed methodology seeks to estimate the determinants of past observed oil prices, in the hope that these determinants will also predict future oil prices.

Some other works have examined cross-sectoral impacts of oil shocks. Kilian and Park, 2009, used an SVAR approach to analyze the relationship between returns on U.S. stocks and crude oil demand and supply shocks.[16] Ready, 2018, also analyzed the association of oil shocks with stock returns, using a PR with demand shocks and supply shocks separately specified.[17] Herrera, Karaki, and Rangaraju, 2017, used a FAVAR to analyze the effect of negative oil price shocks on job flows, creation, and destruction using Bureau of Labor Statistics (BLS) employment data.[18]

---

[15] Christiane Baumeister and James D. Hamilton, "Structural Interpretation of Vector Autoregressions with Incomplete Identification: Revisiting the Role of Oil Supply and Demand Shocks," *American Economic Review*, Vol. 109, No. 5, 2019.

[16] Lutz Kilian and Cheolbeom Park, "The Impact of Oil Price Shocks on the U.S. Stock Market," *International Economic Review*, Vol. 50, No. 4, 2009.

[17] Robert C. Ready, "Oil Prices and the Stock Market," *Review of Finance*, Vol. 22, No. 1, 2018.

[18] Ana María Herrera, Mohamad B. Karaki, and Sandeep Kumar Rangaraju, "Where Do Jobs Go When Oil Prices Drop?" *Energy Economics*, Vol. 64, 2017.

An I-O technique developed by Baqaee and Farhi, 2019, allows for estimation of the impact of oil price shocks on the U.S. GDP. The I-O model is based on 88 sectors of the U.S. economy, and sector-level total factor productivity estimates are also used.[19] Thus, a sector-by-sector aggregate estimate of the GDP change attributable to first- and second-order effects of narratively identified oil shocks is created. Finally, Wei, 2003, utilized a CGE approach, in contrast with the VAR- and PR-heavy method previously described, to test whether oil shock–induced capital obsolescence was statistically responsible for observed declines in stock market valuations of listed firms.[20] Equity prices and employment are key economic indicators that can have political implications, so the extent of the oil price's impact on them is of key interest for policymakers.

Labor Shocks

Labor resources, and remuneration for their employment, are subject to the same kinds of economic shocks that affect non-human resources. Supply and demand for labor in the DIB may be suddenly shifted due to laborer preferences, immigration or outmigration, or policy changes. Furthermore, the need for several types of highly specialized labor sources in the DIB may expose certain industries and defense capabilities to greater disruptions in response to labor shocks. For example, highly specialized labor pool disruption could degrade readiness at the weapon-system level, such as the AV-8 jet.

Foroni, Furlanetto, and Lepetit, 2018, sought a method for separately identifying labor supply shocks and wage shocks.[21] The approach uses a Bayesian vector autoregression (BVAR) to analyze BLS data series, including employment vacancies, wages, output, the labor force participation rate, and the unemployment rate. Recent developments in labor shock method-

---

[19] David Rezza Baqaee and Emmanuel Farhi, "Productivity and Misallocation in General Equilibrium," *Quarterly Journal of Economics*, Vol. 135, No. 1, 2020.

[20] Chao Wei, "Energy, the Stock Market, and the Putty-Clay Investment Model," *American Economic Review*, Vol. 93, No. 1, 2003.

[21] Claudia Foroni, Francesco Furlanetto, and Antoine Lepetit, "Labor Supply Factors and Economic Fluctuations," *International Economic Review*, Vol. 59, No. 3, 2018.

ologies also manifested from several COVID-19 pandemic analyses. Brinca, Duarte, and Faria-e-Castro, 2020, used a BSVAR model to analyze BLS data.[22] Their model assesses the change in monthly hours worked that was attributable to the shock of COVID-19 lockdowns and reopenings in the United States, separately estimating labor demand and labor supply. Such analyses can help to inform the planning for delivering DIB capabilities under future labor market scenarios. Across the DIB, there is the potential for disruption in production and distribution due to a widespread labor shortage, such as that caused by the COVID-19 pandemic. Alternatively, a widespread change in labor policies, such as minimum wage increases, could propagate differentially through a combination of layoffs and price increases in impacted sectors.

Financial Shocks

Financial conditions can be disrupted by such shocks as increased uncertainty, sudden shifts in credit spreads and availability, and unanticipated market movements, to name a few. Such events can degrade the financial health and operational performance of firms in the DIB. For example, extended timelines could be needed for multiyear procurements and execution of block buy contracts. Financial headwinds may cause slowdowns in improvements and upkeep for capital intensive facilities. Furthermore, there is the potential for ripple effects across firms in securing access to necessary capital during a credit crunch.

VAR and PR have also been used extensively in this subarea of shock analysis. Traditional topline economic health indicators such as output (GDP) and equity prices have been studied extensively. Shiller, 2017, used an event study–type PR to show that lagged equity prices and shock events can predict future equity prices.[23] Gilchrist and Zakrajšek, 2012, examined whether corporate bond credit spreads, using a specially constructed index,

---

[22] Brinca, Duarte, and Faria-e-Castro, 2020.

[23] Robert J. Shiller, "Narrative Economics," *American Economic Review*, Vol. 107, No. 4, 2017.

could predict quarterly GDP in a VAR.[24] The same corporate bond credit spreads are an input variable in the I-O analysis of Bigio and La'O, 2020, utilizing I-O tables from the U.S. Bureau of Economic Analysis.[25] The credit spread financial distortions are associated with a first-order negative effect on the labor wedge and a second-order effect on the efficiency wedge, suggesting that financial shocks spread varying degrees of negative impacts to production across the U.S. economy.

Baker, Bloom, and Davis, 2016, investigated financial policy uncertainty.[26] Their PR model shows a link between policy uncertainty and stock price volatility, reduced investment, and reduced employment. Furthermore, their VAR modeling shows an association between policy uncertainty and declining investment, output, and employment in the macroeconomy.

Other research has investigated the change in other macroeconomic indicators, such as consumption, wages, employment, and credit availability, that is due to financial shocks. Fisher and Peters, 2010, used excess returns to military contractors as a source of presumably macroeconomically exogenous government spending–related financial shock.[27] Utilizing a VAR modeling approach, they estimated the macroeconomic response to these government spending shocks, specifically in terms of output, hours, consumption, and real wages. Chodorow-Reich, 2014, examined the relationship between credit availability and employment growth, utilizing a PR with instrumental variable design to estimate whether exposure to credit limitations had a negative effect on employment at various firms.[28] Costello, 2020, examined spillovers resulting from constrained trade credit channels as a type of financial shock.[29] PR utilizing a difference-in-differences

[24] Simon Gilchrist and Egon Zakrajšek, "Credit Spreads and Business Cycle Fluctuations," *American Economic Review*, Vol. 102, No. 4, 2012.

[25] Saki Bigio and Jennifer La'O, "Distortions in Production Networks," *Quarterly Journal of Economics*, Vol. 135, No. 4, 2020.

[26] Scott R. Baker, Nicholas Bloom, and Steven J. Davis, "Measuring Economic Policy Uncertainty," *Quarterly Journal of Economics*, Vol. 131, No. 4, 2016.

[27] Jonas D. M. Fisher and Ryan Peters, "Using Stock Returns to Identify Government Spending Shocks," *The Economic Journal*, Vol. 120, No. 544, 2010.

[28] Chodorow-Reich, 2014.

[29] Costello, 2020.

design estimates the reduction in the volume of credit available to customers downstream of the supplier suffering the constraint.

Conclusion

After concluding our review, which we narrowed to include trade and agriculture, oil, labor, and financial shocks, it was apparent that the types of shocks that interested us were most commonly analyzed using four key classes of methods: VAR, I-O modeling, CGE models, and various flavors of PR techniques. VAR techniques may include FAVAR, BVAR, SVAR, and BSVAR implementation. Similarly, CGE models generally appear as static models but can sometimes be estimated as dynamic models. PR techniques include several identification strategies with which the reader may be familiar, such as event-study, difference-in-differences, and instrumental variable techniques.

Published academic research generally emphasizes identification of effects on dependent variables via theoretically backed model mechanisms. A DIB modeling capability might implement the modeling strategies that identified these mechanisms, with the intention of predicting the future variations in DIB-salient dependent variables. For example, a regional-level CGE model might predict the effect of future sanctions on macroeconomic indicators in a politically sensitive foreign region. Conversely, an automated VAR model might anticipate future capability gaps in the domestic DIB resulting from real-time innovations in the price of oil, agricultural commodities, or other traded goods. The implementation and/or automation of existing academic macroeconomic modeling techniques represents an opportunity for the DIB to anticipate future economic conditions, and their consequences for capabilities and readiness, both at home and abroad.

Additional Details on Vignettes

SMS Emden Disrupting British Commerce in World War I

At the outset of WWI, German leaders decided that the best use of their navy, too small to challenge the Royal Navy outright, would be to disrupt British trade routes around the globe through attacks on commerce vessels and supply depots. While German U-boats would become the weapon of choice against British shipping, the Germans first employed their fleet of surface cruisers as commerce raiders.[1] The most successful of these cruisers was the *SMS Emden*.

Under command of Captain Karl von Müller, the *SMS Emden* deployed to the Indian Ocean with a single support vessel to wage "cruiser warfare." Its mission: Disrupt enemy commerce and tie down as many warships as possible. Unencumbered by the Squadron, the *Emden* moved quickly and unexpectedly into the Indian Ocean. From its first attack in September through its demise in November 1914, the *Emden* would raid and bombard adversary supply nodes while capturing or sinking 23 vessels, destroying an estimated £5,000,000 of assets (over $800 million in 2020 U.S. dollars). However, direct costs were not the only effect. The raids sent insurance rates for ships skyrocketing, increased regional commodity prices, and induced panic in locals and European leaders.[2] At the peak of the *Emden*'s opera-

---

[1] Javier Ponce Marrero, "Logistics for Commerce War in the Atlantic During the First World War: The German Etappe System in Action," *The Mariner's Mirror*, Vol. 92, No. 4, 2006.

[2] Van der Vat, 1984, p. 119.

tions, the British halted their commercial shipping from Indian Ocean ports, Triple Entente powers delayed convoys to secure more powerful escorts, and a total of 78 Allied warships searched for the *Emden* instead of conducting other naval operations.[3] The psychological impacts were also long-lasting—several South Indian languages over 100 years later contain the word *Emden* to describe a bold or cunning person.[4] Although the Germans were not able to disrupt British shipping enough to turn the war in their favor, German raiders such as the SMS Emden created short but significant effects on British commerce and Triple Entente military operations in the region.

Economic modeling capabilities could have helped inform decisions about the deployment (for Germany) and mitigation (for the Allies) by exploring questions such as the following:

- (Germany) Given the adversaries' global trade networks, economic structure, and military supply chains, where would commerce raiding be most cost-effective?
- (Germany) What is the upper bound of disruption by a single vessel?
- (Germany) What is the marginal value of deploying an additional commerce raiding vessel?
- (Allies) Given the availability of alternative sources and alternative requirements for military assets, how much effort should be diverted toward the defense of trade routes?
- (Allies) To what extent might disruption of civilian-oriented commerce compromise military objectives?

Confederate Industrial and Financial Constraints During the U.S. Civil War

After the Battle of Fort Sumter, the Confederate states were suddenly cut off from the industrial and financial resources of the rest of the Union

---

3 Paul G. Halpern, *A Naval History of World War I*, Annapolis, Md.: Naval Institute Press, 1994, pp. 75–76; Woods, 2020; Van der Vat, 1984, p. 119.

4 Janaka Perara, "Why They Call Cunning People 'Emden,'" *The Island*, November 3, 2011.

and unprepared for a protracted war. Through competent and innovative leadership in the Confederate Ordnance Department—the organization charged with supplying Confederate forces with arms and munitions—the Confederacy created an industrial base that met, although unsustainably at the conflict's end, the military's demand for the tools of war in the face of numerous supply shocks.[5] However, the Ordnance Department was an exception.

The Confederacy's decentralized governance philosophy, extending from senior officials to state leaders to private citizens, left the Confederacy unable to generate sufficient revenue through taxes, bonds, or loans and left it unable to coordinate transportation demands across the South.[6] The Confederacy tried to meet near-term fiscal demands by printing fiat currency, but the large increase in the money supply soon led to a vicious cycle of increasing prices and hoarding essential commodities by private businesses.[7] By 1864, the inflation-induced shortages, exacerbated by degraded transportation networks across the South, left both soldiers and civilians malnourished, underdressed, underpaid, and with low morale.[8] With labor stretched thin between agriculture, industry, and the front lines; supply chains dismantled by Union forces or poor management; and an ineffective financial system that aggravated both issues, the Confederacy could no longer sustain its war effort or the government itself.

---

[5] Adrian T. Marinez, "Mobilizing the Confederate Industrial Base for Total War," master's thesis, Quantico, Va.: U.S. Marine Corps Command and Staff College, Marine Corps University, March 2011; Frank E. Vandiver, "Makeshifts of Confederate Ordnance," *Journal of Southern History*, Vol. 17, No. 2, May 1951.

[6] In addition to a decentralized government, the wealth of the agriculture-based Southern economy was largely illiquid and vulnerable to shocks in cotton trade, which occurred throughout the war. For more information on the monetary policy of the Confederacy, see Eric Nielsen, "Monetary Policy in the Confederacy," *Region Focus*, Fall 2005.

[7] Benjamin M. Washburn, IV, *An Analysis of Confederate Subsistence Logistics*, master's thesis, Wright-Patterson Air Force Base, Ohio: Air Force Institute of Technology, September 1989.

[8] Andrew F. Smith, "Did Hunger Defeat the Confederacy?" *North & South*, Vol. 13, No. 1, May 2011, p. 7.

Confederate leaders faced decisions on how to manage their industrial resources, finances, and transport networks to mitigate shocks and constraints as they presented themselves. Economic modeling capabilities could have helped inform these decisions by exploring questions such as the following:

- At what rate would disruptions to transportation networks ripple through the supply chain?
- What is the latency between labor and resource shortages in DIB and operational impacts? Through which channels do these impacts travel?
- What are the minimum resource requirements for production over various time horizons? How long can they be sustained?
- At what point does inflationary spending to stimulate industrial output become unsustainable?

Contested U.S. Rubber in World War II

Prior to its entry into WWII, the United States received almost the entirety of its rubber supply from British Malaya and the Netherlands Indies, which together produced 90 percent of the world's natural rubber.[9] As early as 1934, U.S. government officials recognized the U.S. dependency on the few rubber-producing islands, as well as their vulnerability to Japanese encroachment in the region.[10] However, due to President Roosevelt's unwillingness to fund stockpiling initiatives preceding and during the 1937–1938 recession to avoid spending deficits, the U.S. government did not authorize widespread stockpiling until 1939, nor did it make substantial efforts to develop alternative resources until U.S. entry into the war in December

---

[9] Rubber Reserve Company, *Report on the Rubber Program, 1940–1945*, Washington, D.C., 1945, p. 8.

[10] Jonathan Marshall, *To Have and Have Not: Southeast Asian Raw Materials and the Origins of the Pacific War*, Oakland, Calif.: University of California Press, [1995] 2020, p. 34.

1941. By the time Japan cut off the East Asian rubber supply in April 1942, the United States had less than a year's supply of natural rubber.[11]

The U.S. government saw synthetic rubber as the primary replacement to the lost East Asian supply, but the small synthetic industry, which contributed less than 1 percent to U.S. rubber consumption in 1941, could not immediately replace, nor was it guaranteed to replace, the lost East Asian supply before the stockpile was exhausted. While the U.S. government debated and financed the construction of synthetic rubber plants, it mitigated stockpile depletion by cultivating imports from South America and Africa, attempting to start a domestic natural rubber industry, and conserving domestic resources, which included reducing civilian consumption and recycling scrap rubber. These mitigations, although with mixed utility, augmented the stockpile from 1942 until synthetic rubber production reached sufficient capacity and manufacturers adapted to the new rubbers. Indeed, by 1944, synthetic rubber production exceeded initial expectations and made up 80 percent of U.S. rubber consumption. Altogether, these efforts provided sufficient rubber to meet all military demands with no loss to operational effectiveness. However, fulfilling military requirements (which were often overstated) also came at the cost of unsustainable reductions to civilian consumption that could not have lasted beyond the war.[12]

While the U.S. government efforts to prepare for and replace the sudden loss of critical military and civilian material were ultimately successful, the many decisions made before and during the global rubber supply shock could have benefited from additional analytical capabilities. For one, data collection and modeling could have identified the centralized rubber supply chain, then answered questions such as the following:

---

[11] FDR's resistance to stockpiling and later appropriations are discussed in Marshall, [1995] 2020, pp. 35–42; development of alternative sources, including the synthetic rubber industry, is discussed in Paul Wendt, "The Control of Rubber in World War II," *Southern Economic Journal*, Vol. 13, No. 3, January 1947.

[12] U.S. Office of the Rubber Director, *Report of the Director of Rubber Programs to the War Production Board*, Washington, D.C.: War Production Board, 1945. An additional year of war and military rubber requirements would have likely led to the removal of some essential civilian transportation, per Wendt, 1947, p. 226.

- Given potential disruption to current supply lines, to what extent could the United States increase imports?
- At what rate could the United States build stockpiles?
- How long would said stocks offer a buffer against shocks?
- What are the relative benefits of domestic supply (natural and synthetic), and at what production rates do they become relevant?
- To what degree could curbing civilian consumption aid the military effort?
- Given current expected OODA cycles, when should these mitigations be activated to have needed effects?
- At what price points do each of the mitigation strategies become relevant?

Disruptions to Germany's Oil Access During World War II

Prior to WWII, Germany relied on imports for 70 percent of its annual oil supply, the vast majority of which came from overseas. German officials recognized the vulnerability of these imports in the event of war and began investing in a self-sufficient, domestic oil industry—centered on synthetic oil production—as soon as the Nazi government took power in 1933. Although it sought to increase crude oil output, a lack of significant reserves made the primary focus synthetic oil—a capability that, with significant cost, converted Germany's rich coal reserves into liquid fuels. Germany also attempted to stockpile oil, but maintaining secrecy and meeting prewar industrial demands received priority. Only a few months' worth of supply was held in reserves just before Germany's invasion of Poland in 1939.[13]

Once the war began, Germany lost access to overseas imports, 60 percent of its annual prewar supply, and shortly thereafter lost access to oil from Russia, which provided just under 10 percent of the German oil supply in 1940. With its burgeoning domestic synthetic industry and impressment of Romania crude oil production, along with severe cuts to civilian consump-

---

[13] U.S. Strategic Bombing Survey, *The Effects of Strategic Bombing on the German War Economy*, Vol. 3, Washington, D.C.: Overall Economic Effects Division, 1945, pp. 73–81.

tion and a reduction in military requirements, Germany absorbed these shocks and even saw record oil supplies by early 1944. While the oil situation was not critical before 1944, the shocks degraded military effectiveness, most notably by restricting pilot training hours and further motorization of German army.[14]

By March 1944, domestic crude and synthetic production provided 70 percent of Germany's annual oil supply, a reversal of its prewar oil position. However, starting in May 1944, the Allied bombing campaign began delivering the fatal shock to the German oil industry, reducing production to just 12 percent of its peak by March 1945. Aviation fuel supply quickly dwindled, grounding most the Luftwaffe's record number of aircraft within months. Fuel consumption for ground forces persisted until stocks were depleted in September and then were cut drastically thereafter, leaving German field officers unable to make proper tactical use of their equipment. Although conscious military action by the Allies induced the final shock, a change in economic conditions, such as labor shortages, inflation, or supply chain disruptions, could have also induced a similar, but perhaps slower, shock to German oil.[15]

German leadership faced key decisions before and after each oil shock. Economic modeling could have helped inform these decisions, exploring the following questions:

- To what extent could Germany increase alternative imports or expand domestic production in response to various shocks?
- At what rate could Germany build stockpiles? How long would they buffer against shocks?
- What are the relative benefits of domestic supply? At what production rates are they relevant?
- At what price points do each of the mitigation strategies become relevant?

- What resilience remains after employing mitigation strategies against shocks?

---

[14] U.S. Strategic Bombing Survey, 1945, pp. 73–81.

[15] U.S. Strategic Bombing Survey, 1945, pp. 73–81.

- How would the impact of strikes on various nodes (kinetic or nonkinetic) spread through supply networks? Over what time horizons?
- Given current expected OODA cycles, what frequency and intensity of disruptions will degrade capacity?

Nationalization and Reprivatization Disrupt Ownership and Management of the British Shipbuilding Industrial Base (1977–1987)

British shipbuilding experienced significant shocks to ownership and management that impacted the industry's ability to deliver ships to the Royal Navy. In the 1970s and 1980s, shipbuilding was one of many British industries and manufactories caught up in changing directions of a larger political-economic environment. Under government by the Labour Party in 1977, the industry was nationalized, meaning that swathes of the industry were brought under the banner of a state-owned enterprise, British Shipbuilding. After the election of the Conservative Party government headed by Margaret Thatcher in 1979, many state-owned companies were lined up to be sold back to the private sector. British Shipbuilding's turn to do so came in 1988.[16]

Amid these to-and-fro domestic political forces, the UK's shipbuilding industry was facing significant global headwinds. East Asian countries, such as Japan and Korea, were manufacturing and exporting cheaper ships. Meanwhile, longer-term changes in commercial shipping patterns had resulted from the oil crises of the 1970s. Finally, the onset of the jet age led to the sunset of all but the last remnants of the transatlantic passenger shipping business.[17] Economic modeling capabilities could help to explore questions such as the following:

---

[16] Alan G. Jamieson, "Losing the Market: Shipbuilding 1918–1990," in Alan G. Jamieson, *Ebb Tide in the British Maritime Industries: Change and Adaptation, 1918–1990,* Liverpool, UK: Liverpool University Press, 2003, pp. 75–80.

[17] Stephen Koepp and Adam Zagorin, "Sailing Off the Deep End: The Shipping Industry Pitches and Yaws Through an Epic Slump," *Time,* Vol. 127, No. 9, March 3, 1986.

- What is the distribution of defense contracts and other business across the domestic and foreign DIB?
- Does that distribution indicate an increased probability of a change in ownership structure?
- Are the operations and timelines of the DIB contracts robust to a change in firm ownership?
- What is the probability that an ally or competitor would nationalize or privatize a segment of its DIB?
- How might such a move affect allied capabilities or the strategic environment?

Iraqi Invasion of Kuwait (1990)

The nearly decade-long Iran-Iraq war left the Iraqi government facing war debt, reconstruction costs, and domestic demands that it could not afford with its annual revenues, 95 percent of which were based on oil exports. The repressive nature of the regime and lack of a formal peace treaty with Iran made foreign investment or credit line extensions unlikely, while the return of soldiers oversaturating the labor force depressed the economy and added pressure for the government to improve living standards after the war. In response to the impending fiscal crisis and expected domestic unrest, the Iraqi government—namely, Saddam Hussein—demanded that Kuwait and other Gulf nations provide Iraq with capital and forgive their wartime debts. Iraq justified these demands as repayment for defending the Arab nations from Iranian expansion. At the same time, Iraq requested that the OPEC nations reduce oil production quotas so that Iraq could increase production without depressing prices. Kuwait and the United Arab Emirates refused to forgive Iraq its war debts, did not provide capital, and stayed above its quota for oil production. Iraq, which asserted historical claims to Kuwait, accused the country of supporting an imperialist-Zionist plot against Iraq, as well as infringing on its sovereignty and stealing its wealth by stealing oil from under its border. Although Kuwait and the United Arab Emirates eventually agreed to stay under their quota, Kuwait stated that it would not yield to Iraqi demands for compensation. To Iraq, Kuwait was unjustly waging an economic war, one that Iraq would not bear as it faced a looming crisis.[18]

On August 2, 1990, Iraqi forces invaded Kuwait. From the Iraqi perspective, Kuwait's resources would allow the country to afford reconstruction efforts, meet domestic demands, and repay its debts within five years.[19] Denouncing the invasion, the UN swiftly applied sanctions and an embargo on Iraqi oil. By December, Iraq was reported to have lost 90 percent of its imports and 97 percent of its exports.[20] Coalition military efforts soon struck valuable targets in Iraq, further constraining the economy, and eventually removed Iraqi forces from Kuwait. The sanctions and effects of the Gulf War left conditions in Iraq, described at one point as a return to the 19th century, below that of preinvasion levels for years to come.[21] From the U.S. perspective, the Iraqi invasion of Kuwait and Gulf War cost the U.S. approximately $100 billion in 2011 dollars and 147 combat deaths and aggravated the ongoing recession with a spike oil prices and increased uncertainty.[22]

Iraqi leaders faced key decisions on how to address the economic difficulties in the country after the Iran-Iraq war, as well as after the invasion of Kuwait and application of UN sanctions. U.S. leaders also faced decisions on when to intervene. Economic modeling capabilities could have helped inform these decisions by exploring questions such as the following:

---

[18] For further detail on Iraqi perspectives leading up to the invasion of Kuwait, see Efraim Karsh and Inari Rautsi, "Why Saddam Hussein Invaded Kuwait," *Survival*, Vol. 33, No. 1, 1991.

[19] Abbas Alnasrawi, "Iraq: Economic Sanctions and Consequences, 1990–2000," *Third World Quarterly*, Vol. 22, No. 2, April 2001, p. 208.

[20] "Standoff in the Gulf; Excerpts from Remarks by Webster and Baker on Embargo's Drain on Iraq," *New York Times*, December 6, 1990, p. A16.

[21] Alnasrawi, 2001, p. 209.

[22] Stephen Daggett, *Cost of Major U.S. Wars*, Washington, D.C.: Congressional Research Service, RS22926, June 29, 2010; Defense Casualty Analysis System, "U.S. Military Casualties—Persian Gulf War Casualty Summary Desert Shield/Desert Storm," Defense Manpower Data Center, webpage, undated; Marc Labonte and Gail Makinen, *U.S. Military Intervention in Iraq: Some Economic Consequences*, Washington, D.C.: Congressional Research Service, RL31585, May 16, 2003, p. CRS-9.

- How vulnerable or sensitive are government revenue sources?
- How long will reserves last given various magnitudes of shock?
- What revenue demands does the government prioritize? What economic consequences stem from this prioritization? Does the government prioritization impose costs or yield benefits for entities outside Iran? What is the latency until these impacts are felt?
- How effective could mitigation efforts be under various conditions?
- What is the cost of intervention at various points? What is the cost of not intervening?

Cornered Markets: China Changed Rare Earth Materials Export Control to Limit Japanese Access During a Diplomatic Dispute (2010)

China's dominance of extraction and processing of rare earth critical materials left Japan vulnerable to the economic shock of export controls. China currently dominates world markets, in both extraction and processing, for certain rare earth materials that are small but crucial inputs in manufactured systems. In 2010, a collision between Chinese and Japanese vessels in disputed waters near the Senkaku Islands escalated into a diplomatic crisis, with one manifestation being an embargo of rare earth materials exports from China to Japan. Chinese officials implicitly implemented the embargo by delaying export and customs control certificates for shipments of rare earth elements that were ready to be shipped to Japan rather than creating an explicit new trade policy. While the matter was resolved in a matter of weeks, the potent implications of rare earth materials as a political-economic bargaining chip were made apparent. A persistent disruption could have caused crippling delays and shortages in Japan's electronics industry.[23]

The global economic outlook for these materials is particularly challenging. Few countries besides China have the ability to produce the industrial-

---

[23] Marc Humphries, *Rare Earth Elements: The Global Supply Chain*, Washington, D.C.: Congressional Research Service, R41347, December 16, 2013.

ready versions of materials such as tungsten and molybdenum. Extraction and refining of the materials is not prohibitively difficult, but it is relatively dirty and dangerous. Additionally, the process requires large upfront capital investment and is subject to the volatility of commodity prices; these factors make the industry particularly amenable to government subsidy and state involvement. China has been more willing and able to pursue these actions than other nations have been.[24,25]

Future DoD decisionmakers will need to identify unique commodities or subcomponents that are dependent on one or a handful of other nations for exports. While rare earth materials are a well-publicized example, there may be other relevant but overlooked examples. Analysis of possible future scenarios might include identifying the predictors and likelihood of an export restriction by single-source producer countries, such as China. Additionally, in the case of a bilateral dispute, decisionmakers would want to anticipate whether other allied or neutral nations might significantly modify their behavior, on both the supply and demand sides. All of these actions would have an impact on global prices and availability for the materials or parts. Economic modeling tools could inform this analysis by answering research questions such as the following:

- What unique commodities, such as rare earth materials, are critical inputs to industrial processes and products and are also produced in only a very small number of countries?
- How large is the typical national demand for these quantities?
- What is the potential for recycling or strategic stockpile? What is the potential for other foreign suppliers to allow the United States to offset hypothetical export restrictions over the short to medium term?
- What is the likelihood that a foreign supplier would enact export restrictions? What factors contribute to that decision?
- What would happen to global markets if the foreign supplier enacted export restrictions? Who would the United States be competing with

---

[24] Silberglitt et al., 2013.

[25] Keith Johnson and Robbie Gramer, "U.S. Struggles to End Reliance on Rare-Earth Minerals from China," *Foreign Policy*, May 25, 2020.

on the demand side? What new sources might emerge on the supply side?

U.S. Budget Control Act of 2013

In 2013, the U.S. Congress failed to reach an agreement on alternative budget cuts, thus triggering "automatic, across the board" budget cuts that came to be known as the budget sequestration. Because the cuts were not targeted or phased, critically important staff and activities were impacted, negatively affecting defense capabilities. GAO found that cancellation of training exercises and furloughs in contracting and acquisition offices had negative impacts on readiness and caused delays in acquisition programs.[26]

In the current medium-term global environment, government budgetary uncertainty and shocks are a common economic reality. For example, if political policy follows the same course postpandemic as it did after the global financial crisis of 2007–2008, budget cuts may be politically expedient in countries that have borrowed substantially to prop up their economies during the pandemic. Furthermore, geopolitical pressures could have upside or downside impacts on defense budgets at home and abroad. Recent increases in European NATO partner defense spending could be considered an upward shock to defense budgets. Consequent budgetary reductions, possibly due to austerity measures or treaty changes, are also plausible.

Future DoD decisionmakers would do well to maintain situational awareness, potentially through an economic modeling capability, of the existence and probable magnitude of domestic and foreign budgetary fluctuations. This would include fluctuations that have a direct impact on defense (i.e., the defense budget) and fluctuations that have an indirect impact (e.g., foreign policy, civilian space agencies). The budgetary anticipation would be used to model future impacts on DIB capabilities, readiness measures, and acquisition timelines. It is important to recognize that this anticipation would involve both the domestic budget and relevant budgets of allies or

---

[26] U.S. Government Accountability Office, *Sequestration: Documenting and Assessing Lessons Learned Would Assist DOD in Planning for Future Budget Uncertainty*, Washington, D.C., GAO-15-470, 2015.

competitors to maintain an updated view of global defense spending. Specifically, economic modeling capabilities might help to understand the following budgetary research questions:

- Can we predict the effect of budgetary constraints (domestic and foreign) on the DIB?
- To what extent is the domestic DIB exposed to domestic budget fluctuations?
- To what extent is the domestic DIB exposed to foreign ally budget fluctuations?
- To what extent are the DIB and supply chain of foreign allies exposed to foreign budget fluctuations?
- What is the probability and magnitude of the effect on specific budget items or departments if cuts or expansion were to occur?

Sanctions Against Russia Force the United States to Initiate an Acquisition Program to Replace RD-180 Rockets (2014)

Russian actions annexing Crimea in 2014 prompted a response by the U.S. Congress that included a package of economic sanctions. Concerned that the targets of the sanctions could continue to profit from or influence the United States via purchases of Russian-made RD-180 rocket engines, Congress sought to restrict their import.[27] These engines power the Atlas V launch vehicle, which is regularly used for space-related missions. As of 2014, there was no viable alternative to power Atlas V, meaning that a ban on imports of RD-180 engines would have left the United States with a finite existing supply.

Originally, Congress intended for the RD-180 to be phased out by 2019. Due to schedule slippage in the development of domestic replacements, the RD-180 is expected to be used until at least 2022. The RD-180 engine technology was cheap and reliable, making it a staple of national security

---

[27] Melody Petersen, "Congress OKs Bill Banning Purchases of Russian-Made Rocket Engines," *Los Angeles Times*, December 14, 2014.

and defense space launch missions. As the United States aerospace industry attempts to manufacture a replacement, there is no guarantee that it will be able to replicate all the desirable technical features.[28]

Assuming that the supply of imported RD-180 engines will soon be exhausted, the United States has a few options moving forward in the short term, DoD and NASA could use other launch vehicles not powered by RD-180 engines. However, because launch vehicles have varying technical properties, such as payload, mission requirements may be partially unmet. This case demonstrates that the intersection of policy shocks with R&D timelines is an important economic phenomenon to consider in the context of the DIB.

In the medium- to long-term future, it is highly likely that the United States' global foreign policy strategy will include deploying sanctions as an economic tool. As such, situations similar to that of the RD-180 may emerge again. In those cases, DoD decisionmakers may benefit from economic modeling to answer questions such as the following:

- Can we probabilistically identify policies or actions taken by foreign DIB suppliers that will likely result in sanctions being imposed?
- What threshold of confidence in the sanctions prediction could be the basis for a domestic decision to invest in R&D activities to replace an imported component (e.g., RD-180s) in advance of the rogue foreign policy actions?
- What is the expected capability, capacity, and time horizon that domestic firms would need in order to succeed at R&D activity to develop a replacement for the imported component?
- How can we compare the probability of sanctions imposition with the probability of R&D success to trigger R&D on a replacement part or capability?

---

[28] Matthew Bodner, "Can SpaceX and Blue Origin Best a Decades-Old Russian Rocket Engine Design?" *MIT Technology Review,* June 26, 2019.

The Effects of Energy Price Shocks on Russian Government Spending (2014–2016)

In the years prior to 2014, Russia's oil and gas sales were a staple income source for the federal government, accounting for 50 percent of annual federal revenue.[29] While increased oil prices following the global financial crisis allowed for growth in Russian military spending, a surplus of global oil between 2014 and 2016 sent prices downward. The average global oil price, over $100 per barrel at the start of 2014, fell 50 percent by January 2015, then bottomed out at just over $30 in February 2016.[30] The global price shock decreased Russia's oil and gas revenues by 48 percent between 2014 and 2016, ultimately leading to a 25 percent decline in federal revenue over the same period.[31] While oil prices fell, Russia also faced international economic sanctions following its invasion of Crimea and support to pro-Russian separatists in Eastern Ukraine. With the oil shock and sanctions, the value of the ruble suffered. By the end of 2016, a ruble could buy only half as much relative to the U.S. dollar as it could two years prior. Unwilling to turn to foreign lenders or spend foreign currency reserves for fear of further destabilizing the ruble, Russian officials had to look inward to balance the budget.[32]

For the first two years after the shock began, Russia prioritized national defense spending and the defense industry. Russia reduced total federal expenditures by 14 percent between 2014 and 2016, mostly across domestic

---

[29] RAND analysis of Russian Ministry of Finance, "Federal Budget of Russian Federation, 1992–2020," webpage, March 12, 2021. Russian budget figures for each year were converted to 2014 rubles using the consumer price index for Russia found at Organisation for Economic Co-operation and Development, "Consumer Price Index: All Items for Russian Federation [RUSCPIALLMINMEI]," webpage, March 30, 2021.

[30] Francesco Grigoli, Alexander Herman, and Andrew Swiston, *A Crude Shock: Explaining the Impact of the 2014–16 Oil Price Decline Across Exporters*, Washington, D.C.: International Monetary Fund, Working Paper No. 17/160, July 18, 2017.

[31] RAND analysis of Russian Ministry of Finance, 2021.

[32] James Dobbins, Raphael S. Cohen, Nathan Chandler, Bryan Frederick, Edward Geist, Paul DeLuca, Forrest E. Morgan, Howard J. Shatz, and Brent Williams, *Extending Russia: Competing from Advantageous Ground*, Santa Monica, Calif.: RAND Corporation, RR-3063-A, 2019.

and social accounts, while keeping national defense spending above its 2014 mark.[33] Officials also targeted the defense industry directly, issuing 685 billion rubles (554 billion in 2014 rubles) in debt forgiveness to Russian defense companies in 2016.[34]

Cuts to domestic and social spending accounts alone, however, did not compensate for the increased defense budget in the face of revenue reductions. To balance the budget deficit each year, officials drew from the Russian Reserve Fund—a capital stockpiling program started in 2008 that retained surplus oil and gas revenues to support government spending in case of an economic shock or budget deficits.[35] The reserve mitigated the shock's impact on the defense budget and other spending priorities until it was nearly depleted at the end of 2017.[36] Russian officials decided against further cuts to domestic and social spending and instead reduced defense spending below 2014 levels for the rest of the decade. In turn, Russia slowed procurement of naval vessels and various aircraft to prioritize other capabilities such as air defense and unmanned aerial vehicles.[37] Future procurement plans under Russia's ten-year State Armament Plan, released in 2017, were also curtailed.[38] While initially spared the shock's impact, Russia's

---

[33] RAND analysis of Russian Ministry of Finance, 2021.

[34] These write-offs are included in the Ministry of Finance's topline national defense budget for 2016. Because the write-offs represented defense expenditures in earlier years, we treat the sum of loan forgiveness as separate from the 2016 defense budget. See Keith Crane, Olga Oliker, and Brian Nichiporuk, *Trends in Russia's Armed Forces: An Overview of Budgets and Capabilities*, Santa Monica, Calif.: RAND Corporation, RR-2573-A, 2019.

[35] Russia began collecting reserve funds in 2004 under a single Stabilization Fund, which was split into the Russian Reserve Fund and National Welfare Fund in 2008. The Russian Reserve Fund was designed to cover government expenses above revenues, while the National Welfare Fund was designed to cover Russia's pension system.

[36] Vladislav Inozemtsev, "Business as Usual: Russia Exhausts Its Reserve Fund," *Eurasia Daily Monitor*, Vol. 15, No. 8, January 19, 2018.

[37] Julian Cooper, "Russian Military Expenditure in 2017 and 2018, Arms Procurement and Prospects for 2019 and Beyond," Pembroke College, Oxford: University of Oxford Changing Character of War Centre and the Axel and Margaret Ax:son Johnson Foundation, February 2019.

[38] Andrew S. Bowen, *Russian Armed Forces: Military Modernization and Reforms*, Washington, D.C.: Congressional Research Service, IF11603, July 20, 2020.

military industrial ambitions became a secondary concern to economic stability and development in the country.

Economic modeling capabilities might help to understand the following budgetary research questions:

- To what extent is the domestic budget vulnerable to external economic shocks that affect key revenue sources?
- To what extent is the domestic DIB exposed to domestic budget fluctuations?
- To what extent do capital stockpiles provide resilience against domestic budget fluctuations that are due to an external economic shock? To what extent do they provide resilience against fluctuations that are due to subsequent shocks?

COVID-19 Lockdowns for Foreign Contractors Delay Australian Naval Acquisitions (2020)

The COVID-19 pandemic unfolded as an exogenous disruption affecting every national DIB across the globe. Australia's DIB faced a challenge qualitatively different from many North American or European countries. Its defense acquisition depended on foreign suppliers that were under completely different lockdown regimes. Specifically, the Australian Navy's submarine and frigate acquisition programs were delayed because of the inability of European designers to work. British and French government restrictions prevented designers there from working on the Australian projects.[39] This disruption happened at a critical juncture for the two acquisition programs, complicating the already delay-prone transfer from the foreign design phase to the domestic production phase.[40]

Similar effects can be anticipated in the event of future natural disasters. For example, a major earthquake in Japan could significantly disrupt busi-

---

[39] Anthony Galloway, "Coronavirus Could Force Delay in $45b Warship Program," *Sydney Morning Herald*, October 26, 2020.

[40] Andrew Tillett, "Navy's New $45b Warships Face Two-Year Delay," *Australian Financial Review*, September 15, 2020.

ness for American suppliers, and vice versa for Japan if a major earthquake struck Silicon Valley or Southern California. While the timing of these shocks is inherently unpredictable, the propagation of their effects can be anticipated. Economic modeling can inform this process in both general terms and in the specifics of higher-likelihood events (e.g., earthquakes on known fault lines, eruptions of active volcanoes) in both domestic and foreign locales.

DoD decisionmakers would benefit from quantitative models and tools that are easily updated with real-time data as the scenario unfolds. In terms of economic modeling, research questions might include the following:

- What is the likelihood of exogenous disruption to foreign contractors (e.g., natural disaster, pandemic) that could cause delays that propagate to the domestic DIB?
- What is the likely duration of plausible exogenous disruption scenarios?
- What foreign firm capabilities and capacity are also present in domestic firms?
- What are the costs of onshoring services for the duration of an exogenous disruption?

Technical Details on Iran Sanctions Case Study

This appendix contains technical information to support the analysis presented in Chapter Four. It presents details surrounding each methodological approach employed in the case study of Iranian sanctions. The appendix is organized as follows: Main sections correspond to each of the three branches of analysis: I-O analysis, VAR models, and our examination of trade flows. Each section contains three subsections. The first subsection describes the data used in the analysis, including data sources and, if applicable, variable transformation processes and descriptive statistics. The second subsection describes in detail the methodological approach itself. Finally, the third subsection presents the complete set of results, along with an interpretation of the findings.

Input-Output Analysis

Data

We obtained 2011 I-O data from the Statistical Center of Iran.[1] The Statistical Center of Iran appears to produce I-O tables once every ten years, making 2011 the most recent available. In particular, we leveraged data on inter- and intrasectoral economic flows for the 99 sectors that make up the Iranian economy, as well as the economic value of final demand for each sector. The data set also contains the total requirements matrix (discussed

---

[1] جدول داده ستانده [Statistical Center of Iran], homepage, undated.

in greater detail below), which is derived from the sectoral economic data described above. These data underpin our analysis of the economic effects of complete sectoral shutdowns and a sanction-induced shock to the oil sector. Finally, our I-O analysis makes use of DIBL and DIFL coefficients to identify critical sectors. These coefficients can be derived from the raw sector and product-level data published in the data set; the Statistical Center of Iran performs these calculations and provides the variables as a part of the data set. The two sets of coefficients are described in greater detail below.

Methodology

Our I-O analysis is centered around identifying key sectors according to three separate (though related) metrics: DIBL coefficients, DIFL coefficients, and how a complete sectoral shutdown would affect the value of total economic output in Iran. We also used the model to evaluate how an oil sector shock comparable to what has occurred in recent history would be expected to affect output; we then compared the model predictions with the observed change in Iranian GDP. This component of the analysis is methodologically similar to analyzing the effects of a complete sectoral shutdown; it can be thought of as a scaled version of this exercise.

All three metrics involve the use of intermediate and final production data by sector. *Intermediate output* refers to the goods and services produced in one sector that are used as inputs to the production processes of other sectors. *Final output* denotes output that is consumed "as is" by end users such as households, businesses, and the government. For a given sector, the sum of intermediate and final output equals total sectoral output. Using intermediate and final production data by sector, one can construct what is known as the total requirements matrix. Its coefficients represent, for each sector, the value of total inputs required to produce one dollar of final goods and services. Upon constructing the total requirements matrix, final output and total output can be related through the following canonical Leontief I-O modeling equation:

$$x = Lf \qquad (1).$$

In this equation, x is a vector of the value of total output by sector, L is the total requirements matrix, and f is a vector of the value of final output by sector. The equation illustrates how the model can be used to solve for the economic value of total industry output that is required to meet given levels of final output: simply premultiply the final output vector by the total requirements matrix. This mathematical relationship forms the basis for our metrics; we now discuss each in turn.

The DIBL coefficient for sector j ($DIBL_j$) is computed by summing the elements contained in column j of the matrix L. Given how the L matrix is defined, this measures the increase in total output that would be generated from a one-unit increase in sector j demand. The "backward" portion of the name of this coefficient comes from the fact that it captures the additional output generated via the observed degree of backward supply chain linkages. Due to the nature of how the Leontief I-O model is constructed, only indirect effects arising from backward linkages are captured.[2]

Using a different set of assumptions, one can use sectoral economic flows data to construct a variant of the traditional I-O model that instead captures indirect effects via forward linkages.[3] This variant of the total requirements matrix can be similarly used to compute DIFL coefficients for each sector. An alternative approach to calculating the coefficients is to instead compute them as the row sums of the L matrix.[4] Both sets of coefficients capture the importance of each sector relative to others through calculating how a unit change to sector demand translates to changes in total economy-wide output. What these measures do not account for, however, is the volume of economic activity that occurs in each sector.

For this reason, we estimated the effects on total economic output of a complete sectoral shutdown separately for each sector. This involved a series of before and after comparisons. In each, we reduced a given sector's final

---

[2] Ronald E. Miller and Peter D. Blair, *Input-Output Analysis: Foundations and Extensions*, 2nd ed., New York: Cambridge University Press, 2009.

[3] The Leontief I-O model assumes that producers use inputs in fixed proportions. An alternative method, known as the Ghosh approach, instead assumes that sectors send fixed proportions of their output to those sectors that use it as a production input. This allows the Ghoshian model to capture indirect effects arising from forward supply chain linkages (Alak Ghosh, "Input-Output Approach in an Allocation System," *Economica*, Vol. 25, No. 97, 1958).

[4] Poul Nørregaard Rasmussen, *Studies in Inter-Sectoral Relations*, thesis, Amsterdam: North-Holland Publishing Co.; Copenhagen: Einar Harcks, 1956.

output by 100 percent and used equation (1) above to compute the implied value of total economic output.[5] This number was then compared with the value of total economic output at baseline sector final output—i.e., the value reflected in the 2011 data. This measure reflects the importance of a sector in terms of the combination of its importance in a unit sense and its size relative to other sectors in the economy.

Results

Tables C.1 through C.4 contain the results of our I-O analysis. Table C.1 presents numerical estimates of the effect of a complete sectoral shutdown on the value of total output for the ten most impactful sectors. Our estimate of the national economic effects of a recent sanction-induced decline

TABLE C.1

Top Ten Sectors by Impact of a Sectoral Shutdown on Total Output

Rank	Sector Name	Percentage Change in Total Output
1	Coke- and oil-refining products production	−12.626%
2	Other buildings	−9.354%
3	Extraction of crude oil and natural gas	−9.262%
4	Food production	−8.166%
5	Wholesale and retail, except motor vehicles and motorcycles	−7.435%
6	Residential buildings	−5.726%
7	Production of motor vehicles and other transport equipment, parts, and accessories	−4.865%
8	Services of private residential units	−4.174%
9	Chemical materials and products production	−2.996%
10	Defense affairs	−2.499%

NOTE: Percentage change in total output specifically refers to the percentage change in the economic value of total output.

---

[5] Total output is constructed as the sum of sectoral output.

TABLE C.2

Top Ten Sectors by Normalized DIBL Coefficient Value

Rank	Sector Name	Normalized DIBL Coefficient
1	Oil and fats production	1.765
2	Production of motor vehicles and other transport equipment, parts, and accessories	1.722
3	Production, transmission, and distribution of electricity	1.566
4	Basic aluminum products	1.564
5	Aviculture	1.553
6	Production, repair, and installation of electrical equipment	1.488
7	Basic iron and steel products	1.477
8	Pharmaceutical products, chemicals used in pharmacy and herbal medicinal products production	1.443
9	Production, repair, and installation of fabricated metal products, excluding machinery and equipment	1.434
10	Other base metals and metal casting	1.383

in oil production comes from a scaled version of the calculation underlying the "extraction of crude oil and natural gas" entry in Table C.1. In particular, we reduced the final output by 41.07 percent instead of 100 percent and computed the resulting change in the value of total output, which equals −3.80 percent. Tables C.2 and C.3 display the top ten sectors according to their DIBL and DIFL coefficients, respectively. Both tables report normalized coefficients, meaning that the coefficient values are in relation to the average sector, which takes a value of one. Lastly, Table C.4 presents sector rankings that result from taking a weighted average of the normalized DIBL and DIFL coefficients, where each receives equal weight. As described in Chapter Four, our findings provide quantitative backing for many of the sectors of the Iranian economy that the United States has sanctioned and highlights other areas where future sanctions could be targeted. It is worth emphasizing that similar approaches could be used to identify which sectors contribute most heavily to a given sector's production, as opposed to

TABLE C.3
Top Ten Sectors by Normalized DIFL Coefficient Value

Rank	Sector Name	Normalized DIFL Coefficient
1	Basic aluminum products	2.044
2	Extraction of ferrous metal ores	1.663
3	Coal and lignite mining	1.632
4	Basic iron and steel products	1.575
5	Mining support services	1.561
6	Production of wood and wooden products, cork, straw, and mat weaving, excluding furniture	1.528
7	Aviculture	1.512
8	Warehousing and transportation support activities	1.495
9	Pipeline transportation	1.486
10	Recruitment activities	1.483

total production. Data permitting, the methods can also be applied at the firm level.

Vector Autoregression Analysis

Data

The data used in our VAR models come primarily from two sources: the World Bank and the Central Bank of Iran (CBI).[6] The World Bank World Development Indicators database contains annual data on oil and gas rents, government spending, imports, gross capital formation, GDP, and military expenditures. The data span 1960 to 2019, though some variables are not reported for all years. For example, oil and gas rents data begins in 1970. These data are typically reported in constant 2010 U.S. dollars; we express

---

6 World Bank, "World Bank Open Data," webpage, undated; Central Bank of the Islamic Republic of Iran, "Annual National Accounts," webpage, undated.

TABLE C.4

Top Ten Sectors by the Weighted Average of DIBL and DIFL Coefficients

Rank	Sector Name	Weighted Average
1	Basic aluminum products	1.804
2	Aviculture	1.533
3	Basic iron and steel products	1.526
4	Oil and fats production	1.497
5	Production, transmission, and distribution of electricity	1.476
6	Other base metals and metal casting	1.421
7	Mining support services	1.413
8	Rubber and plastics production	1.374
9	Production of motor vehicles and other transport equipment, parts, and accessories	1.372
10	Paper, paper products, and printing production	1.329

NOTES: Estimates display the weighted average of normalized DIBL coefficients and normalized DIFL coefficients. Each coefficient received equal weight.

each of these variables in log per capita terms using the population data also contained in the World Bank World Development Indicators database.

The CBI data are used primarily for their information on disaggregated government spending. Specifically, we examined health spending, social affairs spending, defense spending, education spending, and economic affairs spending. In the specification that estimates the effects of an oil shock on disaggregated government spending, we used oil and gas value-added data from the CBI to standardize within-specification data sources to the extent possible. Oil and gas value added is defined as the difference between their economic value and the costs of goods and services used in production that are procured from other firms; it is thus conceptually similar to the oil and gas rents variable used in the other specifications. The annual CBI data cover the time period 1960 to 2013. These data were originally reported in constant 2005 billions of rials. We converted these figures to constant 2010 U.S. dollars using the Iranian consumer price index from the World Bank and the U.S.-Iran exchange rates from the International Monetary Fund's International Financial Statistics database.[7]

Finally, some of our specifications incorporate Iran's polity score. This variable is taken directly from the Center for Systemic Peace's Integrated Network for Societal Conflict Research's data page.[8] It is a 21-point index that ranges from –10 to 10. The scale represents a spectrum of governing authority that ranges from autocracies on one end to democracies on the other. Scores from –10 to –6 denote autocracies, scores between –5 and 5 denotes anocracies, and scores from 6 to 10 denote democracies. Table C.5 presents summary statistics for the variables used in our specifications.

Methodology

VARs are dynamic statistical models, meaning that they model how variables change over time. In particular, they empirically assess how a set of variables co-move over a given time frame—i.e., how the variables affect one another contemporaneously and dynamically. We used VARs in our analysis to examine how sanctions (operationalized through a shock to oil and gas rents) have historically affected key economic, military, and political variables of interest to decisionmakers. While we applied the method to national, annual data, the models can also be applied to more-granular data sets (e.g., firm-level data and monthly data).[9]

A general VAR model can be expressed in the following manner:

$$y_t = A_1 y_{t-1} + \cdots + A_p y_{t-p} + \varepsilon_t \quad (2).$$

where y_t denotes a vector of endogenous variables at time t, p is the number of lags in the system, ε_t is an error term, and A_i, $i = 1, \ldots, p$ are matrixes of time-invariant coefficients. We estimated three separate six-variable VAR

---

7   International Monetary Fund, "International Financial Statistics (IFS)," data set, undated.

8   Center for Systemic Peace, "INSCR Data Page," webpage, undated.

9   Vuolteenaho, 2002; Mark Gertler and Peter Karadi, "Monetary Policy Surprises, Credit Costs, and Economic Activity," *American Economic Journal: Macroeconomics*, Vol. 7, No. 1, 2015.

TABLE C.5

Summary Statistics for VAR Variables

Variable	Mean	Standard Deviation	N
World Bank			
Oil and gas rents	1,359.33	897.14	46
Military spending	253.03	243.11	60
Nonmilitary government spending	484.64	249.79	60
Imports	1,048.68	678.62	60
Gross capital formation	1,910.45	990.24	58
GDP	5,664.57	1,680.64	60
CBI			
Oil and gas value added	1,753.88	1,131.63	53
Health spending	25.47	13.71	53
Social affairs spending	41.77	26.93	53
Military spending	189.87	149.16	53
Education spending	36.92	19.16	53
Economic affairs spending	87.13	46.99	53
Polity score	−6.41	3.88	59

NOTES: The World Bank data span 1960–2019; the CBI data cover 1960–2013. All variables aside from polity score are expressed in 2010 U.S. dollars per capita.

systems. In the first, the vector of endogenous variables includes oil and gas rents, military spending, imports, gross capital formation, GDP, and the polity score. The second includes oil and gas rents, military spending, nonmilitary government spending, imports, gross capital formation, and GDP. The third and final specification includes oil and gas value added, economic affairs spending, social affairs spending, health spending, military spending, and education spending. All baseline specifications used a one-year lag.

Our regression models are motivated by leading papers in the literature on estimating the impacts of sanctions on Iran.[10] The specifications listed above can be viewed as excursions from the models contained in these papers; we extended the data used in the literature and studied a slightly different set of variables that better accorded to the present context. We took this approach for several reasons. First, our primary goal was to illustrate how existing, leading approaches can be used complementarily for decision support. Tailoring the specifications outlined in leading published research achieves this purpose. Second, we wished to make explicit the limitations of existing data and methods in providing comprehensive and robust decision support.

We constructed and estimated a large number of models that all drove toward a similar conclusion: Output, military spending, and higher-level political effects constitute the most-relevant outputs that are supported by available data. Documenting changes to military spending over time as a consequence of sanctions, for example, provides valuable information for decisionmakers, but it does not shed light on the potential strategic, operational, and tactical consequences of the predicted spending decline. A small number of studies we surveyed included military spending and political outcome measures as endogenous variables in their models. Given their centrality in demonstrating where the knowledge gap lies, this reinforced the decision to base our models on existing academic practice. Thus, we followed the literature in choosing how to operationalize a sanctions shock. As discussed earlier, while sanctions have been placed on numerous sectors of the Iranian economy, they have largely targeted the oil sector.[11] Accordingly, we treat shocks to oil rents as capturing the consequences of sanctions placed on the Iranian oil sector. Doing so has the added benefit of capturing variation in the magnitude of historical shocks, which would not be cap-

[10] Farzanegan, 2011; Dizaji and Van Bergeijk, 2013; Sajjad F. Dizaji and Mohammad R. Farzanegan, "Do Sanctions Constrain Military Spending of Iran?" *Defence and Peace Economics*, 2019.

[11] This is not surprising given that oil revenues account for the dominant share of government and export revenues in Iran (Farzanegan, 2011).

tured by using an indicator variable that reflects only whether a sanction is in place or not.[12]

We used the VAR estimates to construct impulse response functions (IRFs) that depict the causal effect of an oil shock on other variables over the following five years. The IRFs recursively generate forecasts by drawing on the parameters estimated in equation (2). Specifically, we studied the effects of a one-standard-deviation decrease in oil rents. The key assumption that allows us to identify the causal impact of the shock is that oil rents do not respond to movements in the other endogenous variables within the same period. That is, our identification comes from a Cholesky decomposition in which oil rents are ordered first in the model.[13] This assumption is likely to hold in practice because of oil prices being dictated by world markets, meaning that they are unlikely to be affected by changes in Iran's domestic economy.

Results

Figures C.1 through C.3 plot the resulting IRFs for each of our VAR specifications, along with 68-percent confidence bands.[14] Specifically, each graph shows the response of a given variable to an exogenous one-standard-deviation decrease in oil and gas rents (Figures C.1 and C.2) or oil and gas value added (Figure C.3). The plots are to be interpreted as reflecting the effect on a given variable at a given time horizon relative to the counterfactual in which the shock had not occurred. For example, consider the year

---

[12] There are additional difficulties with using an indicator variable to measure the impacts of sanctions placed on Iran. Because of the frequency and duration of sanctions levied against Iran, an indicator variable is unlikely to exhibit substantial variation over the historical data sample. One approach to overcoming this obstacle is to instead use a variable that captures the relative severity of different sanctions (Dizaji and Farzanegan, 2019).

[13] The order of variables in our description of each specification above reflects the Cholesky ordering that we used in each model.

[14] This is standard practice in the macroeconomics literature, although there is no particular reason motivating this choice. See Valerie A. Ramey, "Identifying Government Spending Shocks: It's All in the Timing," *Quarterly Journal of Economics*, Vol. 126, No. 1, 2011.

FIGURE C.1
The Effect of an Oil and Gas Rents Shock, Specification 1

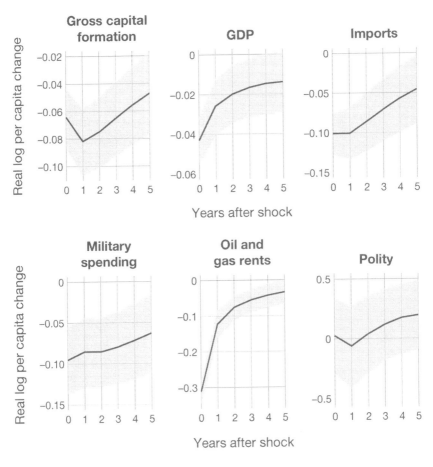

NOTES: Plots depict the response of each variable to a negative one-standard-deviation shock to oil and gas rents. Gray bands represent 68-percent confidence intervals.

two effect on GDP in Figure C.1 and recall that each variable aside from the polity score is expressed in real, log, per capita terms. The value displayed is roughly equal to –0.02, meaning that the log of real GDP per capita is 0.02 units lower at year two following a shock relative to the case in which no shock occurred. Given the approximate relationship between log differences and percentage changes for low numerical values, this means that an

FIGURE C.2

The Effect of an Oil and Gas Rents Shock, Specification 2

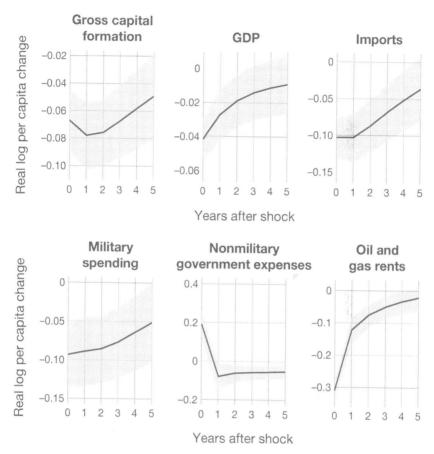

NOTES: Plots depict the response of each variable to a negative one-standard-deviation shock to oil and gas rents. Gray bands represent 68-percent confidence intervals.

oil shock causally reduced real GDP per capita by about 2 percent two years after the shock.

The primary results of interest are the following: First, GDP experiences a significant short-run decline before rebounding over the medium term. This demonstrates that sanctions directed toward Iranian oil and gas activities are effective at creating economic pressure in the near term. Second, military spending decreases substantially and persistently follow-

FIGURE C.3

The Effect of an Oil and Gas Value-Added Shock, Specification 3

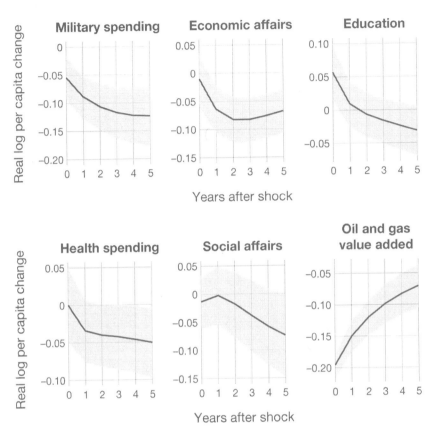

NOTES: Plots depict the response of each variable to a negative one-standard-deviation shock to oil and gas value added. Gray bands represent 68-percent confidence intervals.

ing a decline in oil and gas rents. The effect on military spending is statistically significant for each of the following five years. Notably, the response of military spending is greater in magnitude than the effects on other categories of government spending. This indicates that, historically, military spending has not been spared from the economic pressures arising from sharp declines in oil revenues and, in fact, is relatively more affected than other forms of government spending. Lastly, we found no significant effect of an oil and gas rents shock on Iran's polity score, indicating that the level of democracy in Iran has not historically been affected by movements in the oil and gas industry. Moreover, the point estimate at each horizon is near zero. Consequently, oil and gas sanctions may not be an effective means of spurring this type of governmental change, at least over this time horizon.

International Trade Analysis

Data

Our international trade analysis is largely based on the product-level trade data contained in the UN Comtrade database. In particular, we examined 2011 Iran exports, by HS product code and destination, for traded products that fall within key Iranian economic sectors identified by our I-O analysis. The I-O data from the Statistical Center of Iran contained helpful information on how its economic sector categories corresponded to the ISIC Revision 4 categorization scheme, which were used to match products to sectors. We restricted our attention to 2011 data in order to align the trade analysis with the data underlying our I-O modeling. The data contain information on the quantity, weight, and value (in U.S. dollars) of traded products; we used the value of trade in U.S. dollars to describe trade relationships. Unfortunately, technical issues with the UN Comtrade database during our study prevented us from extending our analysis to consider imports. This was a result of operational challenges that prevented users from conducting data queries beyond a predetermined threshold. The inability to perform large-scale data downloads presented other challenges with the export data we were able to obtain; we describe how we addressed those challenges in the following section. The UN Comtrade database did not contain information on Iranian crude oil and natural gas exports by destination country; we obtained crude oil exports data from the EIA, as published in a 2013 report by the Center for Strategic and International Studies.[15] Crude oil exports data are expressed in thousands of barrels per day and cover trade that occurred between January and September of 2011.

---

[15] Cordesman et al., 2013.

Methodology

For each sector besides extraction of crude oil and natural gas, we first mapped Statistical Center of Iran economic sectors to their ISIC Revision 4 counterparts. Next, we used a crosswalk published by the Organisation for Economic Co-operation and Development Structural Analysis databases team to identify which products, according to their six-digit HS Revision 3 product code, fell under each sector.[16] Each six-digit HS code corresponds to a unique sector. Our plan was to then extract all product-level trade data between Iran and every other nation from the UN Comtrade database separately for each sector and aggregate the data up to the country level. However, this scale of data request was not feasible because of ongoing technical issues with the UN Comtrade database.

To work around the data limitations, we aggregated six-digit HS codes up to the four-digit level. The six-digit codes break out four-digit products into more-specific, narrowly defined goods. This sufficiently reduced the size of our data request, allowing us to extract 2011 Iranian export data. However, doing so introduced measurement error, as HS codes are no longer unique at the four-digit level. That is to say, a given four-digit code may contain some six-digit extensions that correspond to products in our sector of interest and others that do not. We chose to apply three separate filtering thresholds whereby we would only include four-digit HS codes that were composed of at least a certain fraction of relevant six-digit codes. The thresholds we implemented were 50 percent, 75 percent, and 90 percent agreement; we report trade statistics separately for each threshold. The procedure is perhaps best illustrated by way of example: Consider the 90-percent threshold. Suppose that a given four-digit HS code contains ten six-digit extensions. If at least nine out of the ten six-digit extensions map to our sector of interest, then the four-digit product level trade data are included in the analysis. If not, that code is excluded. The procedure thus dictates which four-digit product codes we included in our initial data query. Upon extracting the sets of data for each threshold, we aggregated them to the destination country level. The results of these exercises are reported in the following section.

---

[16] Organisation for Economic Co-operation and Development, "HS to ISIC to End-Use Conversion Key," webpage, undated.

Results

Tables C.6 through C.9 present information on the top export destinations for Iranian products produced in five key economic sectors. The sectors we considered are the following: extraction of crude oil and natural gas; coke- and oil-refining products production; food production; chemical materials and products production; and production of motor vehicles and other transport equipment, parts, and accessories. The statistics are computed according to the procedure outlined in the previous section; we report separate totals for the 50-, 75-, and 90-percent agreement thresholds. All monetary figures are quoted in millions of then-year U.S. dollars. As discussed in Chapter Four, oil export data like those shown in the tables have been used to inform the decision of which nations received temporary waivers exempting them from U.S. sanctions. The corresponding statistics for other

TABLE C.6

Extraction of Crude Oil and Natural Gas and Coke- and Oil-Refining Products Production

Extraction		Refining	
Country	Quantity (in thousands of barrels per day)	Country	U.S. Dollars (millions)
China	550	United Arab Emirates	1,262.2
Japan	327	Singapore	1,251.3
India	310	Indonesia	1,034.3
South Korea	228	South Korea	988.8
Turkey	196	China	683.3
Italy	185	India	522.1
Spain	161	Japan	476.8
Greece	103	Ukraine	218.6
South Africa	80	Iraq	127.9
France	58	Turkey	115.1

SOURCES: Extraction statistics are based on crude oil exports data from the EIA as reported in Cordesman et al., 2013; they cover January through September 2011. Refining statistics are calculated using 2011 UN Comtrade data covering all six-digit HS codes that fall within this sector.

TABLE C.7
Food Production

Country (90%)	U.S. Dollars (millions)	Country (75%)	U.S. Dollars (millions)	Country (50%)	U.S. Dollars (millions)
Iraq	859.7	Iraq	859.8	Iraq	910.3
Afghanistan	306.3	Afghanistan	306.3	Afghanistan	308.0
Turkey	64.4	Germany	76.7	United Arab Emirates	97.7
Germany	60.2	Turkey	64.5	Turkey	96.5
Tajikistan	44.6	United Arab Emirates	45.0	Germany	82.7
Turkmenistan	32.6	Tajikistan	44.6	Russia	79.3
Pakistan	32.2	Turkmenistan	32.6	Tajikistan	47.5
Azerbaijan	29.0	Pakistan	32.2	Pakistan	40.7
Vietnam	28.7	Azerbaijan	29.0	Azerbaijan	37.6
Syria	26.5	Vietnam	28.7	Turkmenistan	35.1

NOTE: Table displays 2011 rankings and corresponding statistics for each agreement threshold.

sectors could be used similarly. More generally, however, the information shown highlights the fact that the costs and benefits attached to any given sanctions action are not constrained to the sender and receiver of the sanctions. As such, sanctions decisions should be and often are based on a wider cost-benefit calculus. How international trade information or modeling is used to inform sanctions or other decisions will, of course, depend on specific goals that policymakers are trying to achieve and the circumstances surrounding those goals.

TABLE C.8

Chemical Materials and Products Production

Country (90%)	U.S. Dollars (millions)	Country (75%)	U.S. Dollars (millions)	Country (50%)	U.S. Dollars (millions)
China	3,460.1	China	3,462.8	China	3,462.8
India	1,777.9	India	1,778.3	India	1,778.3
United Arab Emirates	1,145.4	United Arab Emirates	1,145.5	United Arab Emirates	1,145.5
Turkey	407.3	Turkey	409.3	Turkey	409.3
Afghanistan	233.6	Afghanistan	236.9	Afghanistan	237.0
Belgium	192.3	Belgium	192.3	Belgium	192.3
Pakistan	163.0	Pakistan	163.4	Pakistan	163.4
Netherlands	144.3	Netherlands	144.3	Netherlands	144.3
Iraq	128.9	Iraq	129.2	Iraq	130.4
Indonesia	93.2	Indonesia	93.2	Indonesia	93.2

NOTE: Table displays 2011 rankings and corresponding statistics for each agreement threshold.

TABLE C.9

Production of Motor Vehicles and Other Transport Equipment, Parts, and Accessories

Country (90%)	U.S. Dollars (millions)	Country (75%)	U.S. Dollars (millions)	Country (50%)	U.S. Dollars (millions)
Iraq	210.5	Iraq	218.9	Iraq	218.9
United Arab Emirates	16.4	United Arab Emirates	30.7	Syria	159.8
Venezuela	14.6	Venezuela	14.6	United Arab Emirates	32.2
Russia	11.8	Russia	11.9	Venezuela	14.6
Syria	8.9	Afghanistan	10.9	Russia	11.9
Afghanistan	8.8	Turkmenistan	9.8	Afghanistan	10.9
Turkmenistan	8.6	Syria	9.0	Turkmenistan	9.8
Italy	6.2	Italy	6.2	Italy	6.4
Saudi Arabia	4.7	Saudi Arabia	4.7	France	5.1
France	4.5	France	4.5	Saudi Arabia	4.7

NOTE: Table displays 2011 rankings and corresponding statistics for each agreement threshold.

Abbreviations

ASDA	act-sense-decide-adapt
ATP	Acquisition and Technology Policy
BLS	Bureau of Labor Statistics
BSVAR	Bayesian structural vector autoregression
BVAR	Bayesian vector autoregression
CBI	Central Bank of Iran
CGE	computable general equilibrium
COA	course of action
COVID-19	coronavirus disease 2019
DARPA	Defense Advanced Research Projects Agency
DIB	defense industrial base
DIBL	direct and indirect backward linkages
DIFL	direct and indirect forward linkages
DoD	U.S. Department of Defense
EIA	Energy Information Administration
FAVAR	factor-augmented vector autoregression
GAO	Government Accountability Office
GDP	gross domestic product
HS	Harmonized System
I-O	input-output

IRF	impulse response function
ISIC	International Standard Industrial Classification
JCPOA	Joint Comprehensive Plan of Action
NDRI	National Defense Research Institute
NSRD	National Security Research Division
OODA	observe, orient, decide, act
OPEC	Organization of the Petroleum Exporting Countries
PR	panel regression
R&D	research and development
SME	subject-matter expert
SVAR	structural vector autoregression
UN	United Nations
VAR	vector autoregression
WWI	World War I
WWII	World War II

References

Acemoglu, Daron, Ufuk Akcigit, and William Kerr, "Networks and the Macroeconomy: An Empirical Exploration," *NBER Macroeconomics Annual*, Vol. 30, No. 1, 2016, pp. 273–335.

Alam, Md Rafayet, and Scott Gilbert, "Monetary Policy Shocks and the Dynamics of Agricultural Commodity Prices: Evidence from Structural and Factor-Augmented VAR Analyses," *Agricultural Economics*, Vol. 48, No. 1, 2017, pp. 15–27.

Albino, Vito, Carmen Izzo, and Silvana Kühtz, "Input–Output Models for the Analysis of a Local/Global Supply Chain," *International Journal of Production Economics*, Vol. 78, No. 2, 2002, pp. 119–131.

Alnasrawi, Abbas, "Iraq: Economic Sanctions and Consequences, 1990–2000," *Third World Quarterly*, Vol. 22, No. 2, April 2001, pp. 205–218.

Bakas, Dimitrios, and Athanasios Triantafyllou, "The Impact of Uncertainty Shocks on the Volatility of Commodity Prices," *Journal of International Money and Finance*, Vol. 87, 2018, pp. 96–111.

Baker, Scott R., Nicholas Bloom, and Steven J. Davis, "Measuring Economic Policy Uncertainty," *Quarterly Journal of Economics*, Vol. 131, No. 4, 2016, pp. 1593–1636.

Baqaee, David Rezza, and Emmanuel Farhi, "Productivity and Misallocation in General Equilibrium," *Quarterly Journal of Economics*, Vol. 135, No. 1, 2020, pp. 105–163.

Baumeister, Christiane, and James D. Hamilton, "Structural Interpretation of Vector Autoregressions with Incomplete Identification: Revisiting the Role of Oil Supply and Demand Shocks," *American Economic Review*, Vol. 109, No. 5, 2019, pp. 1873–1910.

Berton, Fabio, Sauro Mocetti, Andrea F. Presbitero, and Matteo Richiardi, "Banks, Firms, and Jobs," *Review of Financial Studies*, Vol. 31, No. 6, 2018, pp. 2113–2156.

Bigio, Saki, and Jennifer La'O, "Distortions in Production Networks," *Quarterly Journal of Economics*, Vol. 135, No. 4, 2020, pp. 2187–2253.

Bodner, Matthew, "Can SpaceX and Blue Origin Best a Decades-Old Russian Rocket Engine Design?" *MIT Technology Review*, June 26, 2019. As of March 1, 2021:
https://www.technologyreview.com/2019/06/26/134490/spacex-blue-origin-russian-rd180-rocket-engine-design/

Bond, Craig A., Aaron Strong, Troy D. Smith, Megan Andrew, John S. Crown, Kathryn A. Edwards, Gabriella C. Gonzalez, Italo A. Gutierrez, Lauren Kendrick, Jill E. Luoto, Kyle Pratt, Karishma V. Patel, Alexander D. Rothenberg, Mark Stalczynski, Patricia K. Tong, and Melanie A. Zaber, *Challenges and Opportunities for the Puerto Rico Economy: A Review of Evidence and Options Following Hurricanes Irma and Maria in 2017*, Homeland Security Operational Analysis Center operated by the RAND Corporation, RR-2600-DHS, 2020. As of April 1, 2021:
https://www.rand.org/pubs/research_reports/RR2600.html

Bowen, Andrew S., *Russian Armed Forces: Military Modernization and Reforms*, Washington, D.C.: Congressional Research Service, IF11603, July 20, 2020. As of April 1, 2021:
https://fas.org/sgp/crs/row/IF11603.pdf

Boyd, John R., "The Essence of Winning and Losing," unpublished lecture notes, revised January 1996. As of October 19, 2021:
https://web.archive.org/web/20110723080817/http://www.danford.net/boyd/essence.htm

Brinca, Pedro, Joao B. Duarte, and Miguel Faria-e-Castro, "Measuring Labor Supply and Demand Shocks During COVID-19," St. Louis, Mo.: Federal Reserve Bank of St. Louis, Working Paper 2020-011D, 2020.

Canova, Fabio, Leonor Coutinho, and Zenon G. Kontolemis, *Measuring the Macroeconomic Resilience of Industrial Sectors in the EU and Assessing the Role of Product Market Regulations*, Vol. 112, Luxembourg: Publications Office of the European Union, 2012.

Carvalho, Vasco M., Makoto Nirei, Yukiko U. Saito, and Alireza Tahbaz-Salehi, "DP11711 Supply Chain Disruptions: Evidence from the Great East Japan Earthquake," working paper, 2016.

Center for Systemic Peace, "INSCR Data Page," webpage, undated. As of March 4, 2021:
http://www.systemicpeace.org/inscrdata.html

Central Bank of the Islamic Republic of Iran, "Annual National Accounts," webpage, undated. As of March 4, 2021:
https://www.cbi.ir/simplelist/5796.aspx

Chodorow-Reich, Gabriel, "The Employment Effects of Credit Market Disruptions: Firm-Level Evidence from the 2008–9 Financial Crisis," *Quarterly Journal of Economics*, Vol. 129, No. 1, 2014, pp. 1–59.

Cooper, Julian, "Russian Military Expenditure in 2017 and 2018, Arms Procurement and Prospects for 2019 and Beyond," Pembroke College, Oxford: University of Oxford Changing Character of War Centre and the Axel and Margaret Ax:son Johnson Foundation, February 2019.

Cordesman, Anthony H., Bryan Gold, Sam Khazai, and Bradley Bosserman, *U.S. and Iranian Strategic Competition: Sanctions, Energy, Arms Control, and Regime Change*, Washington, D.C.: Center for Strategic and International Studies, 2013. As of March 1, 2021:
https://csis-website-prod.s3.amazonaws.com/s3fs-public/legacy_files/files/publication/120124_Iran_Sanctions.pdf

Costello, Anna M., "Credit Market Disruptions and Liquidity Spillover Effects in the Supply Chain," *Journal of Political Economy*, Vol. 128, No. 9, 2020, pp. 3434–3468.

Council on Foreign Relations, "International Sanctions on Iran," undated. As of March 3, 2021:
https://www.cfr.org/backgrounder/international-sanctions-iran

Crane, Keith, Olga Oliker, and Brian Nichiporuk, *Trends in Russia's Armed Forces: An Overview of Budgets and Capabilities*, Santa Monica, Calif.: RAND Corporation, RR-2573-A, 2019. As of March 17, 2021:
https://www.rand.org/pubs/research_reports/RR2573.html

Daggett, Stephen, *Cost of Major U.S. Wars*, Washington, D.C.: Congressional Research Service, RS22926, June 29, 2010. As of March 1, 2021:
https://fas.org/sgp/crs/natsec/RS22926.pdf

DARPA—*See* Defense Advanced Research Projects Agency.

Defense Advanced Research Projects Agency, "The Heilmeier Catechism," undated. As of July 14, 2022:
https://www.darpa.mil/work-with-us/heilmeier-catechism

Defense Casualty Analysis System, "U.S. Military Casualties—Persian Gulf War Casualty Summary Desert Shield/Desert Storm," Defense Manpower Data Center, webpage, undated. As of March 4, 2021:
https://dcas.dmdc.osd.mil/dcas/pages/report_gulf_sum.xhtml

De Winne, Jasmien, and Gert Peersman, "Macroeconomic Effects of Disruptions in Global Food Commodity Markets: Evidence for the United States," *Brookings Papers on Economic Activity Fall 2016*, 2016, pp. 183–286.

Dixon, Peter B., Maureen T. Rimmer, and Marinos E. Tsigas, "Regionalising Results from a Detailed CGE Model: Macro, Industry and State Effects in the U.S. of Removing Major Tariffs and Quotas," *Papers in Regional Science*, Vol. 86, No. 1, 2007, pp. 31–55.

Dizaji, Sajjad F., and Mohammad R. Farzanegan, "Do Sanctions Constrain Military Spending of Iran?" *Defence and Peace Economics*, Vol. 32, No. 2, 2021, pp. 125–150.

Dizaji, Sajjad Faraji, and Peter A. G. Van Bergeijk, "Potential Early Phase Success and Ultimate Failure of Economic Sanctions: A VAR Approach with an Application to Iran," *Journal of Peace Research*, Vol. 50, No. 6, 2013, pp. 721–736.

Dobbins, James, Raphael S. Cohen, Nathan Chandler, Bryan Frederick, Edward Geist, Paul DeLuca, Forrest E. Morgan, Howard J. Shatz, and Brent Williams, *Extending Russia: Competing from Advantageous Ground*, Santa Monica, Calif.: RAND Corporation, RR-3063-A, 2019. As of March 30, 2021: https://www.rand.org/pubs/research_reports/RR3063.html

Esri and Li Zhou, "This Map Shows the Full Extent of the Devastation Wrought by U-Boats in World War I," *Smithsonian Magazine*, May 7, 2015. As of March 1, 2021: https://www.smithsonianmag.com/history/map-shows-full-extent-devastation-wrought-uboats-world-war-i-180955191

Farzanegan, Mohammad Reza, "Oil Revenue Shocks and Government Spending Behavior in Iran," *Energy Economics*, Vol. 33, No. 6, 2011, pp. 1055–1069.

Fink, Sheri Lee, *Five Days at Memorial: Life and Death in a Storm-Ravaged Hospital*, New York: Crown Publishers, 2013.

Fisher, Jonas D. M., and Ryan Peters, "Using Stock Returns to Identify Government Spending Shocks," *The Economic Journal*, Vol. 120, No. 544, 2010, pp. 414–436.

Foroni, Claudia, Francesco Furlanetto, and Antoine Lepetit, "Labor Supply Factors and Economic Fluctuations," *International Economic Review*, Vol. 59, No. 3, 2018, pp. 1491–1510.

Galloway, Anthony, "Coronavirus Could Force Delay in $45b Warship Program, *Sydney Morning Herald*, October 26, 2020. As of March 1, 2021: https://www.smh.com.au/politics/federal/coronavirus-could-force-delay-in-45b-warship-program-20201026-p568l3.html

Gertler, Mark, and Peter Karadi, "Monetary Policy Surprises, Credit Costs, and Economic Activity," *American Economic Journal: Macroeconomics*, Vol. 7, No. 1, 2015, pp. 44–76.

Ghosh, Alak, "Input-Output Approach in an Allocation System," *Economica*, Vol. 25, No. 97, 1958, pp. 58–64.

Gilchrist, Simon, and Egon Zakrajšek, "Credit Spreads and Business Cycle Fluctuations," *American Economic Review*, Vol. 102, No. 4, 2012, pp. 1692–1720.

Grigoli, Francesco, Alexander Herman, and Andrew J. Swiston, *A Crude Shock: Explaining the Impact of the 2014–16 Oil Price Decline Across Exporters*, Washington, D.C.: International Monetary Fund, Working Paper No. 17/160, July 18, 2017. As of April 1, 2021:
https://www.imf.org/en/Publications/WP/Issues/2017/07/18/A-Crude-Shock-Explaining-the-Impact-of-the-2014-16-Oil-Price-Decline-Across-Exporters-44966

Halpern, Paul G., *A Naval History of World War I*, Annapolis, Md.: Naval Institute Press, 1994.

Hamilton, James D., "Historical Causes of Postwar Oil Shocks and Recessions," *The Energy Journal*, Vol. 6, No. 1, 1985, pp. 97–116.

Heginbotham, Eric, Michael Nixon, Forrest E. Morgan, Jacob L. Heim, Jeff Hagen, Sheng Tao Li, Jeffrey Engstrom, Martin C. Libicki, Paul DeLuca, David A. Shlapak, David R. Frelinger, Burgess Laird, Kyle Brady, and Lyle J. Morris, *The U.S.-China Military Scorecard: Forces, Geography, and the Evolving Balance of Power, 1996–2017*, Santa Monica, Calif.: RAND Corporation, RR-392-AF, 2015. As of October 18, 2021:
https://www.rand.org/pubs/research_reports/RR392.html

Herrera, Ana María, Mohamad B. Karaki, and Sandeep Kumar Rangaraju, "Where Do Jobs Go When Oil Prices Drop?" *Energy Economics*, Vol. 64, 2017, pp. 469–482.

Humphries, Marc, *Rare Earth Elements: The Global Supply Chain*, Washington, D.C.: Congressional Research Service, R41347, December 16, 2013. As of March 1, 2021:
https://fas.org/sgp/crs/natsec/R41347.pdf

Inozemtsev, Vladislav, "Business as Usual: Russia Exhausts Its Reserve Fund," *Eurasia Daily Monitor*, Vol. 15, No. 8, January 19, 2018. As of April 1, 2021:
https://jamestown.org/program/business-usual-russia-exhausts-reserve-fund/

International Monetary Fund, "International Financial Statistics (IFS)," data set, undated. As of March 4, 2021:
https://data.imf.org/?sk=388DFA60-1D26-4ADF-B505-A05A558D9A42&sId=1479329132316

"Iran Oil: U.S. to End Sanctions Exemptions for Major Importers," BBC News, April 22, 2019. As of March 1, 2021:
https://www.bbc.com/news/world-middle-east-48011496

Jamieson, Alan G., "Losing the Market: Shipbuilding 1918–1990," in Alan G. Jamieson, *Ebb Tide in the British Maritime Industries: Change and Adaptation, 1918–1990*, Liverpool, UK: Liverpool University Press, 2003.

Johnson, Keith, and Robbie Gramer, "U.S. Falters in Bid to Replace Chinese Rare Earths," *Foreign Policy*, May 25, 2020. As of March 1, 2021: https://foreignpolicy.com/2020/05/25/china-trump-trade-supply-chain-rare-earth-minerals-mining-pandemic-tensions/

Karsh, Efraim, and Inari Rautsi, "Why Saddam Hussein Invaded Kuwait," *Survival*, Vol. 33, No. 1, 1991, pp. 18–30.

Kelly, Justin, and Mike Brennan, "OODA Versus ASDA: Metaphors at War," *Australian Army Journal*, Vol. VI, No. 3, Summer 2009, pp. 39–51. As of March 1, 2021: https://researchcentre.army.gov.au/sites/default/files/aaj_2009_3.pdf

Kilian, Lutz, "Exogenous Oil Supply Shocks: How Big Are They and How Much Do They Matter for the U.S. Economy?" *Review of Economics and Statistics*, Vol. 90, No. 2, 2008, pp. 216–240.

Kilian, Lutz, "Not All Oil Price Shocks Are Alike: Disentangling Demand and Supply Shocks in the Crude Oil Market," *American Economic Review*, Vol. 99, No. 3, 2009, pp. 1053–1069.

Kilian, Lutz, and Cheolbeom Park, "The Impact of Oil Price Shocks on the U.S. Stock Market," *International Economic Review*, Vol. 50, No. 4, 2009, pp. 1267–1287.

Koepp, Stephen, "Sailing Off the Deep End: The Shipping Industry Pitches and Yaws Through an Epic Slump," *TIME*, Vol. 127, No. 9, March 3, 1986.

Labonte, Marc, and Gail Makinen, *U.S. Military Intervention in Iraq: Some Economic Consequences*, Washington, D.C.: Congressional Research Service, RL31585, May 16, 2003. As of March 1, 2021: https://digital.library.unt.edu/ark:/67531/metadc815424/

Lee, Iona Hyojung, "Industrial Output Fluctuations in Developing Countries: General Equilibrium Consequences of Agricultural Productivity Shocks," *European Economic Review*, Vol. 102, 2018, pp. 240–279.

Li, Minghao, Edward J. Balistreri, and Wendong Zhang, "The U.S.–China Trade War: Tariff Data and General Equilibrium Analysis," *Journal of Asian Economics*, Vol. 69, 2020, Art. 101216.

Marinez, Adrian T., "Mobilizing the Confederate Industrial Base for Total War," master's thesis, Quantico, Va.: U.S. Marine Corps Command and Staff College, Marine Corps University, March 2011. As of January 5, 2021: https://apps.dtic.mil/sti/pdfs/ADA600828.pdf

Marrero, Javier Ponce, "Logistics for Commerce War in the Atlantic During the First World War: The German Etappe System in Action," *The Mariner's Mirror*, Vol. 92, No. 4, 2006, pp. 455–464.

Marshall, Jonathan, *To Have and Have Not: Southeast Asian Raw Materials and the Origins of the Pacific War*, Oakland, Calif.: University of California Press, [1995] 2020.

Miller, Ronald E., and Peter D. Blair, *Input-Output Analysis: Foundations and Extensions*, 2nd ed., New York: Cambridge University Press, 2009.

Miskimon, Christopher, "How the German Cruiser *Emden* Terrorized Allied Shipping in World War I," *The National Interest*, March 5, 2020. As of March 1, 2021:
https://nationalinterest.org/blog/buzz/
how-german-cruiser-emden-terrorized-allied-shipping-world-war-i-129697

Nadali, Davide, "Sieges and Similes of Sieges in the Royal Annals: The Conquest of Damascus by Tiglath-Pileser III," *Kaskal*, Vol. 6, 2009.

Nielsen, Eric, "Monetary Policy in the Confederacy," *Region Focus*, Fall 2005. As of March 1, 2021:
https://www.richmondfed.org/-/media/richmondfedorg/publications/
research/econ_focus/2005/fall/pdf/economic_history.pdf

Office of the Secretary of Defense, *Military and Security Developments Involving the People's Republic of China, 2020*, Washington, D.C., September 2020. As of December 18, 2020:
https://media.defense.gov/2020/Sep/01/2002488689/-1/-1/1/2020-DOD-
CHINA-MILITARY-POWER-REPORT-FINAL.PDF

Organisation for Economic Co-operation and Development, "HS to ISIC to End-Use Conversion Key," webpage, undated. As of March 1, 2021:
https://www.oecd.org/sti/ind/ConversionKeyBTDIxE4PUB.xlsx

Organisation for Economic Co-operation and Development, "Consumer Price Index: All Items for Russian Federation [RUSCPIALLMINMEI]," webpage, March 30, 2021. As of April 1, 2020:
https://fred.stlouisfed.org/series/RUSCPIALLMINMEI

Perara, Janaka, "Why They Call Cunning People 'Emden,'" *The Island*, November 3, 2011. As of March 1, 2021:
http://pdfs.island.lk/2011/11/03/p13.pdf

Petersen, Melody, "Congress OKs Bill Banning Purchases of Russian-Made Rocket Engines," *Los Angeles Times*, December 14, 2014. As of March 1, 2021:
https://www.latimes.com/business/
la-fi-russian-rocket-ban-20141213-story.html

Ponce, Javier, "Commerce Warfare in the East Central Atlantic During the First World War: German Submarines Around the Canary Islands, 1916–1918," *The Mariner's Mirror*, Vol. 100, No. 3, 2014, pp. 335–348.

Ramey, Valerie A., "Identifying Government Spending Shocks: It's All in the Timing," *Quarterly Journal of Economics*, Vol. 126, No. 1, 2011, pp. 1–50.

Ramey, Valerie A., "Macroeconomic Shocks and Their Propagation," Chapter 2 in John B. Taylor and Herald Uhlig, eds., *Handbook of Macroeconomics*, Vol. 2, Amsterdam: Elsevier, 2016, pp. 71–162.

Rasmussen, Poul Nørregaard, *Studies in Inter-Sectoral Relations*, thesis, Amsterdam: North-Holland Publishing Co.; Copenhagen: Einar Harcks, 1956.

Ready, Robert C., "Oil Prices and the Stock Market," *Review of Finance*, Vol. 22, No. 1, 2018, pp. 155–176.

Rose, Adam, Gbadebo Oladosu, and Shu-Yi Liao, "Business Interruption Impacts of a Terrorist Attack on the Electric Power System of Los Angeles: Customer Resilience to a Total Blackout," *Risk Analysis: An International Journal*, Vol. 27, No. 3, 2007, pp. 513–531.

Roth, Jonathan P., *The Logistics of the Roman Army at War*, Leiden, Netherlands: Brill, 1998.

Rubber Reserve Company, *Report on the Rubber Program, 1940–1945*, Washington, D.C., 1945.

Russian Ministry of Finance, "Federal Budget of Russian Federation, 1992–2020," webpage, March 12, 2021. As of April 1, 2021:
https://minfin.gov.ru/ru/statistics/fedbud/

Schott, Peter K., "One Size Fits All? Heckscher-Ohlin Specialization in Global Production," *American Economic Review*, Vol. 93, No. 3, 2003, pp. 686–708.

Shatz, Howard J., and Nathan Chandler, *Global Economic Trends and the Future of Warfare: The Changing Global Environment and Its Implications for the U.S. Air Force*, Santa Monica, Calif.: RAND Corporation, RR-2849/4-AF, 2020. As of October 18, 2021:
https://www.rand.org/pubs/research_reports/RR2849z4.html

Shiller, Robert J., "Narrative Economics," *American Economic Review*, Vol. 107, No. 4, 2017, pp. 967–1004.

Shlapak, David A., David T. Orletsky, Toy I. Reid, Murray Scot Tanner, and Barry Wilson, *A Question of Balance: Political Context and Military Aspects of the China-Taiwan Dispute*, Santa Monica, Calif.: RAND Corporation, MG-888-SRF, 2009. As of October 6, 2021:
https://www.rand.org/pubs/monographs/MG888.html

Silberglitt, Richard, James T. Bartis, Brian G. Chow, David L. An, and Kyle Brady, *Critical Materials: Present Danger to U.S. Manufacturing*, Santa Monica, Calif.: RAND Corporation, RR-133-NIC, 2013. As of October 18, 2021:
https://www.rand.org/pubs/research_reports/RR133.html

Smets, Frank, and Rafael Wouters, "Shocks and Frictions in U.S. Business Cycles: A Bayesian DSGE Approach," *American Economic Review*, Vol. 97, No. 3, 2007, pp. 586–606.

Smith, Andrew F., "Did Hunger Defeat the Confederacy?" *North & South*, Vol. 13, No. 1, May 2011. As of January 5, 2021:
https://andrewfsmith.com/wp-content/themes/wooden-mannequin/pdf/HungerArticle.pdf

Sondhaus, Lawrence, *German Submarine Warfare in World War I: The Onset of Total War at Sea*, London: Rowman & Littlefield, 2017.

"Standoff in the Gulf; Excerpts from Remarks by Webster and Baker on Embargo's Drain on Iraq," *New York Times*, December 6, 1990, p. A16.

Stock, James H., and Mark W. Watson, "Vector Autoregressions," *Journal of Economic Perspectives*, Vol. 15, No. 4, 2001, pp. 101–115.

Tai, Yew Seng, Patrick Daly, E. Edwards Mckinnon, Andrew Parnell, R. Michael Feener, Jedrzej Majewski, Nazli Ismail, and Kerry Sieh, "The Impact of Ming and Qing Dynasty Maritime Bans on Trade Ceramics Recovered from Coastal Settlements in Northern Sumatra, Indonesia," *Archaeological Research in Asia*, Vol. 21, March 2020, Art. 100174.

Taleb, Nassim Nicholas, *The Black Swan: The Impact of the Highly Improbable*, Incerto Vol. 2, New York: Random House, 2007.

Taleb, Nassim Nicholas, *Antifragile: Things That Gain from Disorder*, Incerto Vol. 3, New York: Random House, 2012.

Tillett, Andrew, "Navy's New $45b Warships Face Two-Year Delay," *Australian Financial Review*, September 16, 2020. As of March 1, 2021:
https://www.afr.com/politics/federal/navy-s-new-45b-warships-face-two-year-delay-20200915-p55vpq

Uboat.net, "U-Boat War in World War One," webpage, undated. As of March 3, 2021:
https://uboat.net/wwi/

UN Comtrade Database, homepage, undated. As of March 3, 2021:
https://comtrade.un.org/data/

U.S. Department of Defense, *Summary of the 2018 National Defense Strategy of the United States of America*, Washington, D.C., 2018. As of March 1, 2021:
https://dod.defense.gov/Portals/1/Documents/pubs/2018-National-Defense-Strategy-Summary.pdf

U.S. Energy Information Administration, homepage, undated. As of March 3, 2021:
https://www.eia.gov/index.php

U.S. Government Accountability Office, *Sequestration: Documenting and Assessing Lessons Learned Would Assist DOD in Planning for Future Budget Uncertainty*, Washington, D.C., GAO-15-470, May 2015. As of March 1, 2021:
https://www.gao.gov/products/gao-15-470

U.S. Office of the Rubber Director, *Report of the Director of Rubber Programs to the War Production Board*, Washington, D.C.: War Production Board, 1945. As of March 1, 2021:
https://catalog.hathitrust.org/Record/003097418

U.S. Strategic Bombing Survey, *The Effects of Strategic Bombing on the German War Economy*, Vol. 3, Washington, D.C.: Overall Economic Effects Division, 1945.

Van der Vat, Dan, *Gentlemen of War: The Amazing Story of Captain Karl von Müller and the SMS Emden*, New York: Morrow, 1984. As of February 3, 2021:
http://archive.org/details/gentlemenofwaram00vand

Vandiver, Frank E., "Makeshifts of Confederate Ordnance," *Journal of Southern History*, Vol. 17, No. 2, 1951, pp. 180–193.

Vuolteenaho, Tuomo, "What Drives Firm-Level Stock Returns?" *Journal of Finance*, Vol. 57, No. 1, 2002, pp. 233–264.

Washburn, Benjamin M., IV, *An Analysis of Confederate Subsistence Logistics*, master's thesis, Wright-Patterson Air Force Base, Ohio: Air Force Institute of Technology, September 1989. As of January 5, 2021:
https://apps.dtic.mil/dtic/tr/fulltext/u2/a215428.pdf

Wei, Chao, "Energy, the Stock Market, and the Putty-Clay Investment Model," *American Economic Review*, Vol. 93, No. 1, 2003, pp. 311–323.

Welburn, Jonathan William, and Aaron Strong, *Estimating the Impact of COVID-19 on Corporate Default Risk*, Santa Monica, Calif.: RAND Corporation, WR-A173-2, 2020. As of October 6, 2021:
https://www.rand.org/pubs/working_papers/WRA173-2.html

Welburn, Jonathan William, Aaron Strong, Florentine Eloundou Nekoul, Justin Grana, Krystyna Marcinek, Osonde A. Osoba, Nirabh Koirala, and Claude Messan Setodji, *Systemic Risk in the Broad Economy: Interfirm Networks and Shocks in the U.S. Economy*, Santa Monica, Calif.: RAND Corporation, RR-4185-RC, 2020. As of October 18, 2021:
https://www.rand.org/pubs/research_reports/RR4185.html

Wendt, Paul, "The Control of Rubber in World War II," *Southern Economic Journal*, Vol. 13, No. 3, January 1947, pp. 203–227.

Woods, Desmond, "Occasional Paper 91: Invidious Choices—The German East Asia Squadron and the RAN in the Pacific, August to December 1914," Naval Historical Society of Australia, October 6, 2020. As of February 3, 2021:
https://www.navyhistory.org.au/tag/sms-emden/

World Bank, "World Bank Open Data," webpage, undated. As of March 4, 2021:
https://data.worldbank.org/

جدول داده ستانده [Statistical Center of Iran], homepage, undated. As of March 4, 2021:
https://www.amar.org.ir/%D8%AF%D8%A7%D8%AF%D9%87%D9%87%D8%A7-%D9%88-%D8%A7%D8%B7%D9%84%D8%A7%D8%B9%D8%A7%D8%AA-%D8%A2%D9%85%D8%A7%D8%B1%DB%8C/%D8%AD%D8%B3%D8%A7%D8%A8-%D9%87%D8%A7%DB%8C-%D9%85%D9%84%DB%8C-%D9%88-%D9%85%D9%86%D8%B7%D9%82%D9%87%D8%A7%DB%8C/%D8%AC%D8%AF%D9%88%D9%84-%D8%AF%D8%A7%D8%AF%D9%87-%D9%88-%D8%B3%D8%AA%D8%A7%D9%86%D8%AF%D9%87